Your Weight is NOT the Problem

Your Weight is NOT the Problem

Ditch the diets.
Embrace your worth.
Redefine happiness.

Naomi Holbrook

authors
AND CO.

First published in Great Britain in 2025
by Authors & Co.
www.authorsandco.pub

Copyright © Naomi Holbrook 2025

Naomi Holbrook asserts the moral right to be identified as
the author of this work in accordance with the Copyright,
Designs and Patents Act 1988.

ISBN 978-1-917623-03-2 (paperback)

Medical Disclaimer
This book contains general information about medications
and treatments. The information is not advice, and should
not be treated as such. Do not substitute this information for
the medical advice of physicians. The information contained
in this book is based on the personal and professional
experiences of the author. Always consult your doctor for
yours and your family's individual needs.

Contents

The Old Narrative

Introduction

She stood staring at the remnants of another failed attempt at a healthy weekend. The empty bottles of wine, takeaway containers, and discarded chocolate wrappers were more evidence of a battle she felt she was losing yet again. As she gazed at the mess, a familiar wave of shame washed over her again.

She had promised herself *this* time would be different; she had promised herself this time *she* would be different. This time, she would stick to her diet. But here she was, once again, feeling defeated, alone, and full of regret. It wasn't just about the food; it was about *what* the food represented. It was about the years of struggle, the constant battle, the endless cycles of hope and despair, the countless diets that had all ended the same way. She felt like a failure, trapped in a body that seemed to want to betray her at every turn.

She felt consumed by the constant debilitating cycle, which was now impacting all areas of her life.

She was me, and I am guessing that because you have picked up this book to read, she is *you,* too.

I want you to know something. I understand. I do. I see the tears you've cried in the dark all alone; I see the way you look at yourself in the mirror when no one else is watching you; I see the mask you wear for everyone else to see; I see the bitterness of self-reproach, I see the hopelessness that creeps in when the scales don't budge or, worse still, when the number goes up. I see the pure exhaustion you carry from the mental and emotional energy spent on counting calories, tracking every morsel of food, trying to be 'good', one moment denying yourself the foods you love, then the inevitable guilt when you succumb to the cravings and overindulge to the point where you feel sick; both physically and emotionally. I see the pain of feeling like you're not good enough, of wondering why it seems so easy for everyone else and yet, so frustratingly impossible for you.

I see all of this because I have been there too. I know exactly what it's like to feel trapped in your body and your mind, to feel like no matter how hard you try, it's never enough. I know the frustration of trying every diet under the sun only to end up in the same place or further away. I know the crushing weight of feeling like a failure.

I felt those feelings, too, for close to three decades.

But I'm here to tell you that you are not a failure. And more importantly, there is a way to break free from these feelings. There is a solution, one that you might not have considered yet. It's not another diet, not another restrictive and boring meal plan, not another exhausting exercise routine. It's something different, something deeper, and it's something that I know can work for you because it has worked for me and for hundreds of women who have been coached and mentored by me, too.

You see, the problem isn't you. The problem is the approach you are taking. Diets and quick fixes only address the symptoms of weight gain, *not* the root cause. They don't consider the deep emotional ties you have to food, the complex relationship you have formed with it since your earliest days, the way you use it to cope with stress, to soothe your anxieties, to fill the voids you may feel in your life. Diets don't address the underlying beliefs and patterns that drive your behaviours. They don't take into consideration the way you are marketed and sold on a daily basis.

That's where my solution comes in. I have gone from truly loathing myself and what I see when I look in the mirror to fully accepting and loving myself, from my thoughts about food being completely obsessive and chaotic to them taking a healthy back seat.

This method is about changing the way you think about food, the way you relate to your body, and the way you see yourself through your own eyes. It's about healing from the inside out, breaking free from the cycle of diets and guilt, and finding the path to true, lasting health and happiness, enabling you to manage your weight effectively and create freedom.

I know you're thinking you've already tried *everything*; I thought that too, which is what kept me stuck in a destructive and exhausting cycle for far too long.

I know you're also thinking this sounds too good to be true because I know you have been sold so many false promises of this before, as was I. I would have been skeptical, too, had I not experienced the life-changing results for myself, and I don't use the word life-changing lightly. But once I started to understand the real reasons behind my lifelong eating habits, once I started to address the emotional and psychological aspects of my relationship with food and myself, everything changed, and I believe it can change for you too.

I want you to take a moment to imagine waking up in the morning with a clear, calm mind and not feeling dread about stepping on the scales or opening your wardrobe to scour through and see what you can still fit into. Imagine enjoying *every* meal without any guilt, without shame, without that little voice in your head constantly telling you you're a failure. Imagine feeling at complete peace and ease with your body, feeling strong, healthy, and confident. This isn't a fantasy; this isn't a life *other* people get to live; it's possible for you, too, and I want to show you how.

I'm going to be honest with you throughout this book and our journey together, and that starts with a caveat: this journey won't be easy, but it is *simple*. You may have some resistance; I will explain more about this later. It will require you to look inside yourself to confront some of the emotions and beliefs that have been holding you back all these years, but I wholeheartedly promise you that it will be totally worth it. A resounding message from the women I have coached and mentored is they wish they had discovered this method years ago to have saved them from wasting so much time, money, and energy.

The difference this time is you won't be doing it alone. I will be with you *every* step of the way, guiding you, supporting you, and cheering you on.

You've already taken the first step by picking up this book, for which I wish to thank you. That in itself shows courage, determination, a willingness, and a desire to change, and in both my professional and personal experience, those are the exact qualities you need to succeed. So, let's take this journey together. Let's explore a new way of thinking, a new way of living, and, most importantly, a new way of being.

You may not believe this yet, but you *do* truly deserve to feel happy, healthy, and at peace with yourself and your body. You deserve to break free from a lifetime of diets, emotional eating, and poor body image. You deserve to live a life that isn't dominated by food or your weight, and more importantly, you can.

I know that you may feel you are beyond help and think there is something deeply wrong with you; I can assure you that you aren't, and there isn't. Many of the women who have worked with me felt these feelings before they discovered what you are about to discover, too.

I want you to know that I believe in you. Now, it's time for you to start believing in yourself.

So, let's get started.

As you turn the pages of this book, you will learn more about my personal journey and how I discovered the true path to managing my weight and lasting health and happiness. You will find tried, tested, and proven tools and techniques to help you change your relation-ship with food, strategies to overcome emotional eating and drinking, and insights into the psychological and emotional aspects of weight loss.

We will delve into the science behind why diets do not yield long-term success and explore the powerful connection between emotions, thoughts, beliefs, and, importantly, eating habits. You will learn how to listen to your body effectively, nurture yourself without turning to food or alcohol, and create a life that is truly fulfilling and joyful!

This is not a quick fix, but it is a lasting one. It's not about perfection; it's about progress. It's about learning to love and respect yourself, treating your body with kindness and compassion, and finding balance and harmony in all aspects of your life.

Firstly, I know you may be wondering why you should trust me, and I promise I will share more throughout the book, but for now, I want you to know you are in the safe hands of an expert.

I am a Certified Nutrition and Weight Management Coach who has helped hundreds of women trapped in a cycle of emotional eating and the debilitating existence of the diet merry-go-round to live a life of freedom and peace but previous to that, I was a young girl and then a woman who spent most of her life on/off a diet, hating how she felt and looked and her inability to control her weight, her eating habits and her physical, mental and emotional health.

I was either dramatically restricting the food I ate or completely out of control and eating everything in (and out of) sight.

My poor relationship with my body and myself spanned nearly three decades, and I truly believed, through all my failed attempts, it was just who I was destined to be for the rest of my life.

Breaking free from the constraints of dieting and emotional eating is a truly transformative journey that will bring about no end of benefits, positively impacting every facet of your life, not to mention those around you. I have seen this time and time again with the women who have worked with me; their relationships improved, career opportunities enhanced, and so much more.

From someone who previously struggled with all these issues, being liberated from the ongoing cycle has led to a profound sense of freedom, self-love, and inner calm and peace in my own life.

Constant dieting, a deeply disordered relationship with food that I had conveniently justified to myself as completely 'normal', and my poor body image occupied a significant portion of my thoughts, with constant calculations of calories, constant tracking of foods, and constant guilt over my 'bad' choices. This mental preoccupation was truly exhausting, debilitating, and limiting in so many areas of my life. Something I have only come to fully realise since it is no longer a part of my everyday life.

When you finally break free from this destructive cycle, you will reclaim a vast amount of cognitive energy. No longer feel shackled by the incessant need to track every bite or measure your worth by a number on the scales.

Instead, your thoughts can be redirected toward more meaningful and fulfilling pursuits. The mental freedom you soon experience will allow for increased creativity, productivity, and a general sense of clarity. You can focus on personal growth, hobbies and relationships, experiencing life more fully and richly than ever before.

One of the most profound transformations that occurred for me and the women who have worked with me is the development of a healthier and more positive body image.

Dieting often perpetuates a cycle of self-criticism and dissatisfaction. One may constantly feel that one is not meeting the goals one sets for oneself, resulting in a feeling of constant failure.

Does this sound familiar?

As you move away from these destructive habits, you can finally begin to cultivate a sense of self-acceptance and self-appreciation. You will start to see your body as a vessel of strength, resilience, and beauty rather than all the negativity you have previously viewed it with. This shift in perspective will allow you to love the version of yourself you see in the mirror, whatever your shape or size. You will begin to appreciate your unique features and the incredible things your body can do.

This newly found self-love fosters confidence and a more authentic presence in your daily interactions and endeavors.

If you have been in a tumultuous relationship with food and your body for some time, like I was, the constant stress of adhering to restrictive diets, coupled with the emotional roller coaster of using food or alcohol as a coping mechanism, will most likely have created a chaotic and anxiety-ridden existence where you feel you are in a constant state of survival mode, struggling to catch your breath. I felt like I was on a speeding tread-mill that I couldn't stop.

Breaking free from these patterns brings a sense of calm and peace. Without the pressure of restrictive diets, you will be able to develop a more mindful and balanced approach to eating. You will learn to listen to your body's natural hunger and satiety cues, leading to a much more relaxed and enjoyable relationship with food. This new approach will reduce stress and anxiety, lowering cortisol levels, which in turn impacts your body's ability to lose weight, creating a much more harmonious life.

Without the emotional roller coaster of using food as a coping mechanism, you can find healthier and more sustainable ways to manage your emotions. For example, you might turn to more mindfulness practices, physical activity, or creative outlets to process your feelings, which will further contribute to a sense of stability and grounding.

How would you feel having more time in your life to do the things you love, maybe even the things you don't even know you love?

As I sit here writing the words in this book, I know in my heart this is not something I would have been able to do previously; my brain was filled with so much chaos that my thoughts were distorted and didn't allow for any creativity. I was like a robot programmed to function each day but not to feel, to grow, to expand in all the ways a human being is created to. I also know that I would not have had the self-belief to think of myself as becoming a published author because I had very little belief in any of my abilities. My years of dieting and failing those diets impacted my self-esteem, my decisions, my choices, and my actions in more ways than I ever gave it credit for.

Dieting and emotional eating are mentally draining activities. The constant vigilance required to adhere to a diet, along with the constant emotional turmoil of using food to cope with stress or other emotions, can feel like it leaves little room for anything else, and when you do break free from these habits, you will reclaim a huge amount of mental energy. This newfound mental energy can be channeled into pursuits that truly bring joy and fulfillment. Maybe you will dive back into hobbies you've come to neglect or explore new interests, the energy that once consumed you by dieting and emotional eating can now be used to enhance the quality of your life in countless other ways.

Women who have worked with me have taken up running marathons, mountaineering, cold water swimming, teaching art classes, and singing in choirs, among many other things. Of course, you don't need to do *any* of these, but maybe there is something out there you have not yet explored that could, in time, become something incredibly fulfilling and meaningful to you.

Furthermore, a clearer mind and a more stable emotional state will better equip you to handle the challenges of everyday life. My increased mental energy has improved my problem-solving abilities and resilience in this ever-challenging, fast-paced world. Once you leave the confines of autopilot and survival mode, you can become more present and engaged in your daily activities, leading you to a richer, more satisfying life experience.

Breaking free from dieting and emotional eating also has significant benefits for physical health. Chronic and prolonged dieting, as I discovered, can often lead to nutritional deficiencies, metabolic issues, and a weakened and compromised immune system. Emotional eating often involves the consumption of large quantities of unhealthy and ultra-processed foods, which can contribute to weight gain, cardiovascular problems, and other health issues.

By adopting a more balanced and mindful approach to eating, you will also improve your overall nutrition and health. You will become more likely to want to choose foods that nourish your body and provide sustained energy rather than feeling you *have* to. This shift can lead not only to better weight management but also to improved metabolic health and a stronger immune system. Regular, balanced meals help maintain stable blood sugar levels, reducing the risk of diabetes and other metabolic disorders.

Additionally, without the stress of dieting and the guilt and shame that come with emotional eating, people are more likely to engage in regular physical activity. Moving your body becomes a source of enjoyment and a way to enhance overall well-being rather than something you dread or a punishment for your food choices. This positive relationship with physical activity further contributes to improved physical health and a greater sense of vitality, especially as one ages.

Overcoming the cycle of dieting and emotional eating fosters emotional resilience and self-compassion. Breaking free from these habits often involves confronting and addressing underlying emotional issues, which can lead to greater self-awareness and emotional intelligence.

You will learn to recognise and address your emotional needs in healthier ways, building resilience to life's challenges. This emotional strength allows you to navigate stress, setbacks, and difficulties with greater ease and grace. You will become more adept at handling your emotions without resorting to food or alcohol as a coping mechanism.

As you will see throughout this book, self-compassion plays a crucial role in this transformation. By letting go of the harsh self-criticism associated with dieting failures and emotional eating episodes, you will cultivate a kinder and more forgiving relationship with yourself. You'll learn to treat yourself with the same compassion and understanding you would offer to a dear friend or a loved one.

This self-compassion enhances your overall well-being and further encourages a positive cycle of self-care and emotional health.

Dieting and emotional eating, I found, can truly isolate you from your social circles. The fear of eating in social settings, the anxiety over food choices, and the shame associated with emotional eating can often create barriers to authentic connections and social enjoyment.

Breaking free from these habits opens the door to more genuine and joyful social interactions. You can fully participate in social events without the burden of food-related or body image-related anxieties. You can enjoy meals with friends and family, savouring the experience and the company without guilt or stress. This freedom enhances your social life, deepening relationships and creating lasting memories.

Moreover, the improved self-confidence and self-love that come with overcoming dieting and emotional eating enable you to be more authentic and present in your relationships. You can connect with others on a deeper level, fostering more meaningful and fulfilling connections.

The benefits of breaking free from dieting and emotional eating, as you can already see, are far-reaching and transformative. From reclaiming mental energy and finding freedom in daily thoughts to loving the version of yourself you see in the mirror and experiencing a calmer, more peaceful life, the positive impacts are profound. Enhanced physical health, emotional resilience, self-compassion, and authentic connections further enrich the journey. Embracing a balanced and mindful approach to eating and self-care opens the door to a life of greater joy, fulfilment, and well-being.

As we embark on this transformative journey together, I want you to know that it is possible. My big promise to you is that change, healing, and a new way of living are possible. And it starts right here, right now, with you.

I invite you to be open-minded, to leave all your past experiences behind for now, and to take action along the way. I know you're busy and that life is constantly pulling you in different directions, but if you stay with me, I truly believe you won't regret it.

I am encouraging you to take small, simple action steps.

So sit down, take a deep breath, and let's begin.

Chapter One

Why Diets Don't Work!

In the quest for the 'ideal' body, millions of women worldwide embark on diets each year, lured by the promise of rapid weight loss, better health, and, ultimately, happiness. Yet, despite the billions of pounds currently spent on diet programs, pills, and related products, the majority of those who diet find themselves trapped in a vicious cycle of weight loss and regain.

For many, the pursuit of thinness becomes an obsession, overshadowing their lives and impacting their self-worth. But why do diets fail so consistently? To answer this, I'm going to delve into the very nature of dieting; I'm going to share my own personal and somewhat painful journey and my professional experience as a Certified Nutrition and Weight Management Coach. I am going to explore the lucrative industry that profits from it and shed light on the psychological toll it takes on individuals, particularly women who often bear the brunt of continuous societal pressure to conform to unrealistic body standards.

The diet industry is a beast. Its global market value exceeds $250 billion and is projected to double in the next ten years! This figure encompasses everything from weight loss programs and meal plans to diet books, supplements, injections, and even surgery.

Many weight loss companies have become household names and big brands, each promising a unique solution to the age-old problem of weight loss: points, syns, free food, and meal replacement shakes. But what is the business model behind these companies, and why does it seem that so few people achieve lasting success?

The answer I have discovered lies in the very design of these programs. Diet clubs and companies rely on repeat customers to sustain their business. The majority of their revenue comes not from new dieters but from returning customers who have regained the weight they initially lost. This phenomenon, known as "yo-yo dieting" or "weight cycling," is so common that it has become the norm rather than the exception.

Studies have shown that up to 95% of people who lose weight on a diet will regain it within five years, and many will end up weighing more than they did before they started dieting. This cycle of hope, failure, and return is what keeps the diet industry thriving, but as I have learned, only too well can have a hugely detrimental impact, both psychologically and physically, on the individual.

Moreover, the marketing strategies of many diet companies are designed to exploit vulnerabilities. They target you at your most vulnerable moments—after the holidays, before summer, or at the start of a new year—when the pressure to lose weight can feel at its peak. The messaging often plays on insecurities, promising that weight loss will lead to happiness, confidence, and success. However, many dieters painfully discover this fallacy over time.

Are you being set up to fail?

Dieting is all too often portrayed as a simple equation of calories in versus calories out. Yet, the reality of sustainable weight loss is far more complex than this, especially as we age and then add to that the challenges and hormonal roller coaster that menopause can bring!

Weight loss strategies that may have 'worked' in your twenties and thirties will certainly not work after this.

Your body is biologically programmed to resist weight loss. When you restrict your calorie intake, your body naturally perceives it as a threat to its survival. In response, it will slow down your metabolism, increase your hunger hormones, and decrease the production of the leptin hormone that makes you feel full. This is one of the many reasons you may have found it increasingly difficult to stick to a diet over time, leading to the inevitable "cheat days" that spiral into full-blown relapses, or as you may have been inclined to call it in the past "falling off the wagon".

But the psychological impact of dieting goes way beyond just physical cravings. Dieting, as I have found, both personally and professionally, can become an all-consuming mental and emotional battle. Constantly thinking about food, counting calories, and worrying about your weight can lead to anxiety, depression, prolonged low mood, and even eating disorders.

The very act of dieting can erode your self-esteem, making you feel like a failure when, as a human being, of course, you will inevitably slip up. This is compounded by the societal pressure to be thin, which disproportionately still affects women.

To better understand the toll that dieting can take on you, I am going to share some of my personal experience, I am now a fifty-year-old woman in menopause who previously spent over twenty-five years of my life in a never-ending cycle of restrictive diets and over-consumption of food.

My long and exhausting journey with dieting began in my early teenage years when I first became aware of my changing body in a way that felt like it was not entirely my own. Like many young girls going through puberty, I was heavily influenced by images of thin, seemingly perfect young women in magazines and on television. I compared myself to my peers at school, who all seemed to be slimmer and naturally more athletic in comparison to me.

I also started to observe my own Mother, who was then in her early forties, attempting a plethora of different diet fads and meal plans. I often saw her skip meals in the pursuit of being happy with her weight. These rituals appeared to increase in the lead-up to our annual holiday each year.

Reflecting on this as an adult and with the personal and professional knowledge I now have, I do believe that she also had issues with her body image, which took up space in my subconscious thoughts, too.

I remember feeling deeply uncomfortable in my own body, dreading any form of physical activity at school that required me to wear a P.E. kit, and feeling like I was bigger than all the other girls. Looking back at the photos, I was far from it, but that was how I felt at that moment and for many years to come.

Body image issues among adolescent girls can be an incredibly complex topic, shaped by a mix of societal, familial, and personal influences. In my own experience at a competitive all-girls school, where there was an emphasis on excelling in sports alongside academia, the feeling of pressure to conform to certain body ideals felt somewhat relentless.

In environments like that, where every girl is running cross-country or playing netball in those tight, green polyester gym knickers (which, let's be honest, were *not* designed with positive teenage self-esteem or body image in mind), comparisons happened almost instinctively, at least they did for me.

If that's not enough, you add the layers of comparison that happen naturally with peers and siblings. It's like a mental checklist: *"Does she have slimmer legs? Is her hair shinier? Does she have better skin? Can she run a 5K in those ridiculous gym knickers without looking like she's been forced into them like an overspilling sack of potatoes?"*

The comparison between peers often becomes habitual. You're constantly looking to your left and right, not just to see if you're winning the race but also to see how you measure up. Are you as fast as the girl next to you? Do you have the same shape? And sometimes the competition isn't even about fitness—it's about whose green polyester knickers ride up less during the dreaded cross-country race!

It's like a secret competition, except there are no winners, and everyone's as self-conscious as each other.

This comparison mindset doesn't just come from within, though. It can be reinforced by family dynamics—particularly with siblings. If you've got a sibling who is athletic, slender, or excels in some way, it can amplify feelings of inadequacy, even if no one is explicitly comparing you. That internalised sense of rivalry can fuel a lot of the insecurities we carry. You start asking yourself, "Why can't I look like her? Why don't I have *her* confidence? Why don't I look as good in my gym knickers?" (Ah, the scratchy polyester strikes again!)

At the heart of it all, body image issues are often linked to a sense of self-worth. When you're young and still figuring out who you are, it's easy to believe that how you look and how you perform physically are the only things that matter. If you're surrounded by girls who all seem like they have it together (especially when they're casually lunging towards that netball post in those knickers like it's no big deal), it can make you feel like you're falling behind, even though everyone's secretly feeling the same insecurities.

Looking back now, I can laugh at the absurdity of some of it—the fact that someone, somewhere, thought those tight green polyester gym knickers were a *good* idea, for one—but at that moment, those feelings were all too real and painstaking. It's only later in life that you realise everyone else, or mostly everyone was just as preoccupied with their insecurities.

The comparisons and body image struggles that felt so central to your own life in those difficult teenage years were shared burdens, even if no one admitted it at the time.

In essence, we compare ourselves to others because we're all just looking for some measure of reassurance—am I good enough? Am I keeping up? And in a hyper-competitive environment, those comparisons become sharper and more frequent. But, just like those uncomfortable gym knickers, they're rarely a true reflection of who we are or what we're worth.

My very first diet is etched in my own memory. Some three decades later I can still remember I was around fourteen, a tub of meal replacement shakes I had purchased from a local chemist, which I kept hidden in a bag at the back of my wardrobe for fear of my parents discovering it.

I started to skip meals, pretend I had already eaten with a friend, and mix a low-calorie shake in my bedroom when I finally succumbed to the hunger pangs that frequently got too much. It worked at first. I'd lose some weight after checking countless times on the bathroom scales, but as the initial excitement wore off and the powdery synthetic taste started to repulse me, along-side the constant empty feeling in my stomach, I found myself craving what I had restricted. Eventually, I would give in and overeat the foods I had prevented myself from having, and the weight, unsurprisingly, crept back on.

This all too familiar pattern repeated itself over the years and decades, with me trying every diet under the sun: low-carb, low-fat, juice cleanses, intermittent fasting, low-calorie. You name it, I tried it.

I counted calories, points, syn's, and everything in between!

Each time, the result was the same—initial weight loss followed by weight regain, often with more extra pounds added.

As I entered adulthood, the stakes became much higher. I was no longer just dieting or trying to lose weight for my appearance anymore; I was now trying to lose weight for my long-term health and mobility.

In 2009, aged thirty-four and having experienced over twenty years of debilitating back pain and countless medical procedures stemming from curvature of my spine, I required major spinal surgery, including a disc replacement and an anterior lumbar spinal fusion for premature degeneration of my L4/L5 vertebrae.

During this time, I had become increasingly sedentary due to chronic pain, but in hindsight, I was not helping myself with the lifestyle choices I was making.

I had gotten into a cycle of numbing the pain with food and alcohol, 'treating' myself to make me feel better in whatever way I could but leaving me feeling more and more lethargic, less able, and less inclined to want to exercise in any way, shape or form and allowing myself to accept that this was just a part of my life.

Post-surgery was a blur of opioids, caffeine, and cakes being delivered by well-wishing neighbours and friends, which, as thoughtful as they were, didn't help my increasing weight or my recovery.

So, post-rehabilitation and with a renewed sense of hope, I redoubled my efforts and joined various diet clubs, and when they eventually stopped working, I desperately purchased expensive meal plans and started new intensive exercise regimes. But despite my best efforts, when life's challenges crept back, the exercise plans fell away, and the weight would not stay off. With each failed diet, my sense of self-worth slowly diminished. I began to see myself as fundamentally flawed, incapable of achieving the one thing I had been led to believe all along would bring me the lifelong happiness I had been searching for.

By the time I reached my late thirties, I was utterly exhausted, weighing nearly eighteen stone, now clinically obese, and warned by my doctor about the long-term risks of being overweight—especially the onset of Type 2 diabetes.

What I had failed to realise at that time was that I was also starting my transitional journey into menopause, something I had never been educated on or had even been spoken about.

Decades of dieting and abusing my body had left me physically and emotionally drained, and yet, despite not getting the long-term results I so desperately dreamed of, I still returned to the same diet clubs, repeatedly met with the all too familiar welcome from other dieters of 'back again?'.

Albert Einstein memorably said that insanity is doing the same thing over and over again and expecting different results. Looking back, this method, which I repeated, truly was insane, but going back to what I knew always seemed the safest thing to do.

When I added it up, I had spent thousands of pounds on diet programs, slimming products, unused gym memberships, and a wardrobe that spanned from size ten (and my wishful thinking at that time) to size eighteen clothes (which I had by this time filled out), only to find myself further back than where I had started—deeply unhappy with my weight and even unhappier in myself.

The realisation that all these years of dieting had not improved my life, but had instead consumed it, was a painful one. My story is not unique. I know from so many of the women I have coached and mentored they, too, have previously shared a similar experience, trapped in a cycle of dieting, overeating, and self-loathing.

The Diet Culture Trap: Why You Keep Falling for It

Despite the overwhelming evidence that diets don't work, the diet culture and industry continue to thrive. This is partly due to the deeply ingrained societal belief that thinness is synonymous with health, beauty, and success. The media often perpetuates this belief, glorifying slim bodies and demonising fat ones. The medical community reinforces it, emphasising weight loss as the primary solution to health issues rather than focusing on overall physical, mental, and emotional well-being.

Moreover, the diet industry is highly skilled at adapting to changing trends. When one diet falls out of favour, another takes its place, or a company cleverly undergoes a strategic rebrand to bring itself in line with the latest trend. The rise of social media over recent years has only exacerbated this, with influencers and now members of the general public with absolutely no relevant qualifications or professional experience promoting the latest "miracle" diets, supplements, and systems, often with little regard for their effectiveness or more importantly their safety to others.

The result is a constant stream of new diets, fads, and quick fixes, each promising to be the one that finally works. All tactics I frequently succumbed to in my own desperate quest to lose weight and find happiness in my body.

But as I have discovered on my journey, as long as the underlying issues of diet culture and one's complex relationship with food, one's body, and one's self-worth remain unaddressed, every diet is doomed to fail.

To understand why diets don't work, it's important to look at the science of weight regulation. Your body is designed to maintain a stable weight through a complex system of hormones, genes, and brain signals. This system, known as the "set point" theory, suggests that each of us has a natural weight range that our body tries to maintain. When you diet by overly restricting calories, your body interprets it as a threat to its set point. In response, it activates mechanisms to restore the lost weight, such as slowing down your metabolism and increasing your appetite.

This is why dieting often leads to weight regain. Even if you manage to stick to a diet long enough to lose a significant amount of weight, your body will fight to return to its set point when calories have previously been heavily restricted. The more diets you try, the more your body will resist weight loss, making it harder to lose weight in the future. This is one reason why repeated dieting can lead to long-term weight gain.

Furthermore, weight is not solely determined by diet and exercise. The old adage "eat less, move more" completely misses the point and is now well and truly outdated, especially in today's stress-ridden world.

Environmental factors, such as stress, sleep, and social influences, play a significant role. This is why two people can follow the same diet and exercise plan and have completely different results. Dieting often fails to produce lasting results because it doesn't address the complex interplay of other factors that regulate weight.

Breaking Free from the Diet Mentality: A New Approach to Health

If dieting doesn't work, then what's the alternative?

The answer I have found lies in rejecting the diet mentality altogether and adopting a more holistic approach to health and well-being. This means focusing on behaviours and, ultimately, habits that promote well-being rather than just weight loss. It means listening to your body's natural signals of hunger and fullness rather than following arbitrary and restrictive rules about what and when to eat. It means engaging in physical activity that you enjoy rather than forcing yourself to exercise out of guilt or obligation.

This approach, I refer to as "mindful nutrition," is a tried, tested, proven, and healthier alternative to dieting and one of the pillars of the unique S.M.A.R.T. Formula I have created from both my professional and personal experience. Mindful nutrition is based on the principle of tuning into your body's natural cues and eating in response to them rather than external cues like calorie counting, meal plans, or eating windows. It encourages a more positive relationship with food, where all foods are permitted, and there is no guilt or shame associated with eating any food, even foods you may once have deemed to be 'bad'.

Adopting mindful nutrition was truly liberating. However, I initially resisted change, as the very idea of letting go of all the diet rules I had followed for so many years was absolutely terrifying. I had become so obsessed with calorie counting, tracking, counting points, monitoring syn's, scheduling restrictive eating windows, and religiously weighing and measuring everything I ate and myself that *any* alternative felt unknown and somewhat terrifying.

However, as I began to listen to my body rather than my thoughts and eat in a way that felt more natural to me, I noticed a significant shift. Food no longer felt like the enemy. I started to enjoy meals again, savouring the flavours and textures rather than obsessing over calories and tracking points. And more importantly, I began to feel more at peace with my body and in my mind than I had ever done. I stopped categorising food as 'good' or 'bad' and instead looked at what foods made me feel more energized and fuller, increasing my vitality in the long term.

Mindful eating is not a quick fix. It requires unlearning years of diet culture conditioning and rebuilding trust with your body and yourself. But if you have spent what feels like a lifetime dieting, I assure you it will be a truly liberating experience. Mindful eating predominantly shifts the focus from weight loss to overall health and well-being, which is a far more sustainable and fulfilling approach. Weight loss becomes merely a 'side effect' rather than the primary ongoing focus.

Whilst I was so heavily focused on dieting and losing weight, my physical, mental, and emotional health were all rapidly deteriorating.

Until my late thirties, I was on a heavy concoction of prescription medication; high-dosage opioids and anti-inflammatories to manage ongoing chronic back pain, sleeping tablets for insomnia, anti-depressants for ongoing bouts of depression and anxiety, and asthma inhalers, which I had used for twenty plus years and yet there I was still in pain, still depressed, still constantly ill and still struggling with my weight.

A wake-up call if ever I needed it!

What I had failed to realise at that time was that after years of abusing my physical health with dieting and overeating ultra-processed foods was that I was seriously lacking essential nutrients, which had left my body riddled with a multitude of ongoing symptoms. Every new ailment required a new prescription and more medication.

Or so I had believed at that time.

As you may also believe, my failure to diet reflected a weakness, a flaw in my character. However, it was, in fact, a reflection of a flawed approach to weight and health that was the only version I had ever known.

I mistakenly thought I just needed to 'try' harder and find more willpower or motivation. However, through my own research and studies, I finally learned that motivation is not constant, even for the most 'motivated' and successful people.

Your motivation levels will fluctuate based on many external factors, such as mood, stress, sleep, and daily life events. Some days, you may feel highly motivated, but on other days, when you inevitably don't, it can be difficult to stay on track with your weight loss goals. Relying on motivation alone will lead to inconsistency in your efforts and continually 'falling off the wagon'.

You may have been told repeatedly by others, 'You need more willpower,' and I am here to tell you that isn't true. Willpower is finite, a limited resource. It works much like a muscle, which gets slowly fatigued the more you use it. Throughout the day, as you are faced with an enormity of decisions, your willpower depletes.

It may surprise you to learn that you have to make, on average, 33,000 to 35,000 decisions every single day, most of them will happen automatically in your unconscious thoughts, like the times you grab and eat half a packet of biscuits from the cupboard whilst boiling the kettle to make a cup of tea without even thinking about it or how you always grab something out of the fridge to snack on when you start cooking dinner! You can now see how, with all those decisions every single day, this can make it seem increasingly hard to consistently resist temptation or stick to your diet or a meal plan, especially when you are tired, overwhelmed, or stressed.

This is where mindful eating will create consistency even when your motivation levels and willpower are low.

Your constant reliance on motivation and willpower will make the weight loss process feel exhausting, debilitating, and overwhelming, leading eventually to burnout. If you constantly have to resist temptation or push yourself to stay motivated, you may feel mentally and emotionally drained, which no doubt will eventually lead to you giving up.

Maybe you're already there?

Relying on motivation alone doesn't address these external and emotional triggers that can derail even your best efforts.

Achieving lasting weight loss is about long-term behaviour change, not short bursts of effort driven by a new lease of willpower or sporadic motivation. Without a consistent focus on building new, sustainable habits, you will continually revert to old eating or activity behaviours once your willpower weakens or your motivation fades.

The diet industry profits from the belief that thinness is the key to happiness and success, but I found this to be a false promise. Dieting often leads to weight regain, psychological distress, and a negative relationship with food and body image. To break free from this cycle, it's essential to reject the diet mentality altogether, unlearn what you have previously learned, and adopt a more holistic approach to health that focuses on prioritising your well-being over your weight.

For me and countless other women like me, this realisation was bittersweet. It recognized the time, money, and energy wasted on dieting, but it also offered a new beginning—an opportunity to focus on what truly matters: health, happiness, and self-acceptance.

By letting go of diets, you can start to reclaim your life and find joy in food and your body once again.

The journey to self-acceptance is not easy, especially in a world that is constantly reminding you of the need to be thinner, younger, or just a little more perfect. But it is a journey worth taking.

After all, your worth is *not* determined by a number on the scales but by the richness and quality of your life and the love you give and receive.

Diets, with their empty promises and inevitable failures, only continue to distract you from this truth.

It's time to leave it behind and embrace a new way of living—one that honours your body and celebrates your uniqueness.

Chapter Two

The 'Have it Now' Culture vs the Pursuit of Long-Term Happiness

In today's world, we live in what can only be described as a 'have it now' culture. The rapid rise of technological innovations, services like Amazon, Uber Eats, and Deliveroo, and the availability of convenient options have made it easier than ever to satisfy our increasing desires in an instant.

Want a pair of shoes from halfway around the world? No problem, you can order them on Amazon, and they'll be delivered to your doorstep in less than 48 hours.

Craving a pizza at midnight? No problem, Deliveroo can have it to you in under thirty minutes.

Too tired to go to the cinema after a tiring week at work? No problem, Netflix can have that new release on your screen with one click of a button.

With the swipe of a finger, you can satiate your immediate needs and impulses, creating a culture of instant gratification that is constantly feeding (excuse the pun!) into your craving for quick fixes and the belief that you can achieve results overnight.

However, this immediacy I found has a darker more sinister side.

While it may provide you with convenience and a dopamine rush in the short term, it often leaves you feeling deeply unfulfilled in the long run, particularly when it comes to achieving long-term happiness, health, and fulfillment. This is especially evident in areas like weight loss and health, where the promise of quick results and immediate pleasure undermines your ability to stay committed to sustainable and long-lasting habits.

This chapter will explore how this 'have it now' mindset can influence every aspect of life and how my own experiences with ultra-processed food and alcohol have mirrored the instant gratification cycle you may be facing today. By examining your pursuit of quick dopamine hits, the chapter will explore how you can begin to challenge this mindset in pursuit of long-term well-being, happiness, and fulfillment.

We find ourselves living in an unprecedented era of technological advancement where convenience reigns supreme. Online shopping, food delivery apps, streaming services, and instant access to entertainment have now become the norm, somewhat blurring the line between your needs and desires. In just the last two decades, companies like Amazon and Uber have changed the landscape of consumer behaviour.

Growing up, a takeaway or a home movie was a truly special occasion, a rare treat. One day, it became an everyday necessity.

Amazon Prime's promise of next-day delivery has altered our expectations of time. We no longer see waiting as a necessary part of acquiring things; instead, we expect our desires to be fulfilled in a near-instantaneous manner. Uber Eats and Deliveroo have taken this mentality even further by providing near-instant access to indulgent foods. We may have previously savoured these foods for special occasions, but we now have access to them at all hours, with minimal effort required on our part.

In the same way, credit options now allow us to live far beyond our financial means. We no longer have to save up for that new gadget, luxury item, or expensive outfit. We can have it all immediately, whether we can truly afford it or not. And while we may enjoy the rush of receiving our purchases right away, the satisfaction is fleeting, often leaving us with buyer's remorse or debt in the long term.

This pattern of expecting and receiving immediate gratification has permeated nearly every aspect of our lives. The problem with this lifestyle is that it has taught us to prioritise short-term satisfaction over long-term well-being, fostering impatience and making it harder to delay gratification, a key skill for achieving lasting success in areas like health, career, and personal relationships.

At the root of your craving for instant gratification lies dopamine, a hormone and neurotransmitter in your brain associated with pleasure and reward. Every time you receive something you desire—be it an ultra-processed meal, a package, or even a 'like' on social media—your brain releases dopamine, giving you a sense of satisfaction and pleasure. This chemical hit has been proven to be highly addictive, and your brain becomes conditioned to seek out experiences that provide it.

The problem is that human brains are wired to want more. While dopamine may give you that pleasurable feeling in the instant moment, it fades quickly, leaving you in a state of craving for the next hit. This cycle of pleasure-seeking can quickly spiral out of control, particularly when you have so many opportunities to satisfy these desires at your fingertips.

For instance, ultra-processed foods — high in sugar, salt, and unhealthy fats — are chemically engineered to give you a powerful dopamine hit.

Are you familiar with "Once You Pop, You Just Can't Stop!"?

When I struggled with my eating habits, I found myself constantly craving the instant gratification that a chocolate bar or a packet of crisps would provide. It wasn't so much the taste or the satisfaction of eating; it was the quick rush of pleasure that these foods provided me at that moment, much like the high you might get from seeing a handbag in a shop and feeling the intense desire to purchase it on the spot.

Similarly, alcohol became another way for me to access that feeling of pleasure and relief. After a long day or a stressful working week, a glass of wine or a cocktail seemed like the perfect antidote to stress, instantly relaxing me and making me feel better in that moment. But much like with ultra-processed foods, the dopamine high I experienced was short-lived, and I often found myself wanting more, chasing that feeling long after the food and alcohol had been consumed.

What I now know is I had become highly addicted to ultra-processed foods. My palate had become accustomed to them and wanted them more and more. It was a never-ending and somewhat debilitating cycle.

This constant pursuit of the dopamine hit becomes dangerous when it extends into other areas of life. Whether it's eating unhealthy food, shopping impulsively, or even consuming social media, people can become trapped in a cycle of seeking short-term pleasure, often at the expense of their long-term happiness and fulfillment.

The Impact of Instant Gratification on Health and Weight Loss

Nowhere is the impact of our 'have it now' culture more apparent than in the realm of health and weight loss. The continuous promises of quick fixes and instant results in this area are everywhere. Whether it's a new fad diet that claims to help you lose ten pounds in a week, a supplement that promises overnight fat burning, or a weight loss injection that guarantees to reduce your appetite, we are constantly bombarded with solutions that cater to our desire for fast results.

The problem I have found, however, is that health and weight loss do not work that way. Sustainable health improvements require long-term commitment, consistency, and delayed gratification — the complete opposite of what the modern world and our current culture train us to expect, so with this in mind, it is hardly surprising if you keep falling into this trap.

The desire for instant results often leads to poor decisions in the moment, such as opting for crash diets that may result in rapid weight loss but are ultimately unsustainable and tedious. Once the initial thrill of losing weight wears off and the methods you have used are unsustainable, you often find yourself regaining the weight and falling back into all the unhealthy habits you were desperately trying to escape.

I know this all too well from my own experience. When I first started my weight loss journey, I wanted to see fast results. I was impatient and wanted to see the

numbers on the scale drop immediately. I tried everything from juice cleanses to restrictive diets and weight
loss supplements that promised quick results. While I
did lose some weight in the beginning, the progress was
always short-lived, and I found myself falling into the
same old patterns and familiar cycles of overeating and
overindulgence that I had before.

I finally realised that the instant gratification I sought
from food was also reflected in my approach to weight
loss and my health in general. I wanted a quick fix, a
magic pill, just like I wanted the immediate pleasure
that came from eating ultra-processed foods. But weight
loss, like so many other meaningful achievements in life,
requires consistency, patience, and the all-important
ability to delay gratification.

Instead of chasing quick results and expecting overnight success, I chose to shift my mindset toward long-
term health and well-being.

I started focusing on changing my behaviours and
building sustainable habits—eating more whole, nutritious foods, being more active, and being much more
compassionate to myself. While the results weren't
immediate, they were far more lasting and fulfilling.
Over time, I not only lost weight but also developed a
healthier relationship with food and my body.

Our 'have it now' culture extends to food, health, and
all areas of our lives, including material possessions.
The rise of consumerism has made it possible for us
to chase happiness through material goods. We are
constantly bombarded with messages that tell us we

need the latest gadget upgrade, the trendiest clothing, another holiday, or the most luxurious accessories to be happy and fulfilled.

I remember a time when I felt this pull very strongly. Walking through a department store and seeing a beautiful handbag, I would feel an overwhelming urge to buy it. At that moment, it was as if purchasing the handbag would somehow fill a void, providing me with a sense of happiness and satisfaction. While buying the handbag may have given me a rush of pleasure in the short term, that feeling quickly faded, leaving me feeling dissatisfied and wanting more.

Much like with ultra-processed food and alcohol, the satisfaction that comes from buying material goods is fleeting. It provides a temporary dopamine hit, but it doesn't address the deeper underlying issues that may be driving your need for this consumption in the first place.

Whether it's stress, boredom, or a sense of emptiness, we often turn to material goods to fill these emotional voids. But the stark reality is that no amount of shopping, holidays, or acquiring material possessions will bring you the lasting happiness and fulfillment you crave, just like no amount of ultra-processed food or alcohol will either.

The constant pursuit of material goods can have the opposite effect, leaving you feeling emptier and more unfulfilled than ever before. Studies have shown that while material possessions can provide short-term happiness, they do not contribute to long-term well-being.

True happiness and fulfillment come from experiences, relationships, and personal growth. All of these require time, effort, and a willingness to delay gratification.

One key problem with this 'have it now' culture is that it teaches people to prioritise short-term pleasure over long-term happiness. However, lasting happiness and fulfillment come from activities that require patience, persistence, and delayed gratification.

Whether it's building a successful business, maintaining healthy relationships, or achieving long-term health goals, the most meaningful achievements in life, I have discovered, take time. Once you understand and fully embrace this, the journey itself will become so much simpler, not to mention more enjoyable.

Unfortunately, the constant availability of quick fixes and instant gratification makes it harder for you to cultivate the skills needed for this long-term happiness. We've become so accustomed to getting what we want when we want it that we've lost our ability to wait, to work for something over time, and to find satisfaction in the process rather than just the result.

In my journey toward optimal health and well-being, I've come to realise that the pursuit of instant gratification was holding me back from achieving my true potential. Whether it was reaching for 'junk' food when I was stressed or pouring a glass of wine just because it gave me a temporary high, I was constantly chasing short-term pleasure at the expense of my long-term happiness.

It wasn't until I started understanding my thoughts and working on changing my mindset that I began to see significant progress. I stopped focusing on the immediate rewards and started thinking about the long-term benefits of each of my actions, no matter how small. Instead of reaching for ultra-processed food or alcohol when I was stressed, I learned to pause, take a step back, and consider how I would feel afterward.

Would I feel satisfied and fulfilled, or guilty and sluggish? By delaying gratification and choosing healthier options, I not only felt better physically but also experienced a deeper sense of fulfillment overall.

I'm not going to pretend to you that this happened overnight; it didn't. It was a work in progress. I am a continual work in progress, and like any journey to success, I have had plenty of setbacks and lessons to learn along the way.

The same principle applied to other areas of my life. Instead of buying things impulsively, I started thinking more critically about my purchases. Did I need that handbag, or was I just trying to fill an emotional void? By delaying gratification and focusing on what truly mattered, I was able to build a healthier relationship with material possessions and find happiness in experiences and relationships rather than things.

Overcoming this 'have it now' mindset is not easy, especially in a world that is constantly encouraging you to seek out instant gratification but now you are aware of it, look at how many times you are being encouraged a day to buy something you hadn't planned or needed to buy?

The time you drive past the bus stop, there's an advert for the tempting new burger from your favourite fast-food place. The time you walk in to get a takeaway coffee and the barista reminds you of the offer when you add a pastry to your order? The loyalty vouchers you receive on your next supermarket shop to get points on the 'treats' you have been trying so desperately to give up so you can lose weight?

It may feel like a constant battle until you become aware of the way you are being repeatedly tempted and then sold to on a daily basis.

However, it is possible with some conscious effort and a commitment and desire to change. The first step is becoming aware of the ways in which your mindset manifests in your life. Whether it's through food or your approach to your goals like weight loss, you need to initially recognise when you're seeking short-term plea-sure at the expense of your long-term happiness.

Once you become aware of these patterns, you can start to make small yet significant changes. For me, this started with understanding my deeper relationship with food. Instead of continuing to give in to my constant cravings for ultra-processed foods, I began to focus on eating more whole, nutritious meals that would nourish my body in the long term. This didn't mean giving up food for pleasure entirely, which I previously thought was the only way to achieve a healthy weight— I still allowed myself to enjoy some of my favourite foods and drinks in moderation — but I became more intentional about my choices, and I learned to appreciate the satisfaction that came from eating more mindfully.

The same approach can be applied to other areas of your life. Instead of buying things impulsively, take a step back and ask yourself whether the purchase will truly bring you happiness in the long term. When it comes to achieving goals like weight loss or personal growth, I always encourage my clients to focus on the process rather than the end result. Celebrate the small victories along the way and recognise that lasting success will require time and effort.

Finally, it's important to remember that true happiness comes from within. While the instant gratification of certain foods and alcohol can provide temporary pleasure, they will never satisfy the deeper emotional needs that drive these behaviours. By focusing on building meaningful relationships, cultivating personal growth, and pursuing long-term goals, you can create a truly fulfilling life.

Our current culture has undoubtedly made life far more convenient, but it has also made it harder to achieve lasting happiness and fulfillment. The constant pursuit of quick dopamine hits, whether through food, material possessions, or instant results, can leave you feeling emptier and more unfulfilled than ever.

I did not understand how the food industry formulates and engineers these foods in the hope that we will become addicted to them until I became a certified Nutrition and Weight Management Coach and started investing many hours into studying and understanding the science and decisions behind my own choices.

Ultra-processed foods (UPFs) are industrial formulations made mostly from substances extracted from foods combined with artificial ingredients such as preservatives, flavour enhancers, colourings, and emulsifiers. These products include a range of items, from sugary cereals and snacks to fast foods like burgers, fries, and sodas. Though convenient, tasty, and marginally inexpensive, 'UPFs' are designed with a dark twist: they are purposely engineered to be addictive.

This combination of chemicals and additives makes them hyper-palatable, triggering a strong desire to consume more. Food scientists, backed by large corporations, craft these foods to maximize their flavour, texture, and appearance, making them increasingly hard to resist. Food manufacturers strategically mix quantities of salt, sugar, and fat to reach a "bliss point," a term used to describe the optimal combination that pleases the brain's reward system without overwhelming the taste. This bliss point is where the food becomes most satisfying and delicious. However, it also hijacks the brain's natural satiety signals, making it more difficult to stop eating these ultra-processed foods. Trying to use willpower to stop eating these foods when you've already started is a near-on-impossible act.

You've probably discovered this for yourself.

The texture is often engineered and manufactured to be light, crispy, or creamy to further enhance the eating experience. For example, the airy crunch of chips or the creamy consistency of a milkshake creates a sensory appeal that encourages rapid consumption. These textures stimulate the brain's reward centers, urging you to take another bite, sip, or handful.

Chemicals like monosodium glutamate (MSG) and artificial sweeteners are added to amplify the flavour and mask the poor underlying quality of the base ingredients. These additives then overstimulate taste receptors, intensifying the sensory pleasure of eating. Artificial flavours can simulate tastes found in whole foods, making it hard to resist the processed alternatives.

Whole foods contain fibre, which slows digestion and leads to a feeling of fullness. Ultra-processed foods, however, are stripped of fibre, leading to far quicker digestion and the absence of satiety signals. This, in turn, encourages overeating and snacking, as your body doesn't recognise the food in the same way it would recognise whole, natural foods.

Eating ultra-processed foods triggers a cascade of neurochemical reactions, particularly involving **dopamine**, the neurotransmitter responsible for pleasure and reward.

When you consume these highly processed foods, your brain experiences a rush of dopamine. This burst signals pleasure and encourages repetition of the behaviour. However, unlike whole foods, which also provide dopamine but with accompanying nutrients and satiety signals, they offer a disproportionate reward without the same level of satisfaction. This leads to a stronger urge to seek out these foods again to chase the dopamine high.

Ultra-processed foods flood the brain with dopamine in the same way addictive substances like drugs and alcohol do. Over time, the brain builds a tolerance to this, meaning that higher amounts of these foods are needed to achieve the same pleasurable effects. This is why once you start eating them, it feels impossible to stop—they become "cravings" that you need to satisfy deeply rather than mere preferences.

Frequent consumption of ultra-processed foods rewires the brain's reward circuits, making it much harder to exercise self-control; this is where you are most likely telling yourself you lack motivation and willpower, but in fact, your prefrontal cortex, the part of your brain responsible for decision-making and impulse control, becomes far less effective at curbing the impulse to overeat.

This explains why, even though you may *know* these foods are bad for your health and do not help you achieve and sustain your weight loss goals, you still crave and consume them in unhealthy quantities on a regular daily basis.

The very addictive nature of ultra-processed foods I have found is only part of the equation. The fast-food and processed food industries invest billions of pounds in marketing strategies that make it even harder for you to resist these already tempting products. Their goal is to reinforce the addiction cycle and ensure constant consumption.

The global marketing budgets for the processed food and fast-food industries are staggering.

One well-known fast-food chain alone spent nearly **$1.6 billion** on advertising in 2021, targeting children, teenagers, and adults alike. Their marketing strategy often includes commercials, celebrity endorsements, and social media campaigns, all designed to keep their products top of your mind and not to mention the top of your shopping list!

All this whilst Obesity is reportedly the second biggest preventable cause of cancer and costs our National Health Service around £6.5 billion a year. This is already projected to increase to a staggering £9.7 billion by 2050.

The marketing of these ultra-processed foods often taps into emotions like nostalgia, comfort, and happiness. Adverts frequently portray fast food as a reward or a way to bond with family and friends, subtly linking their consumption to positive experiences.

For example, "I'm Lovin' It" is really not just about the food—it's about creating an emotional connection that then drives those cravings.

Ultra-processed foods are often marketed as affordable and convenient, which appeals to our increasingly busy and hectic lifestyles. With slogans like "fast," "easy," or "on-the-go," the marketing reinforces the idea that these products fit seamlessly into your hectic modern-day life. Fast food chains constantly use promotions, loyalty programs, and special deals to ensure you return again and again.

These big food companies often pay to have their products featured in movies, TV shows, and even video games. Sponsorship of sporting events by drinks and snack companies creates an association between fun, entertainment, and junk food, reinforcing the idea that these foods are part of everyday life.

Ultra-processed foods are specifically engineered to be addictive through the strategic use of salt, sugar, fat, flavour enhancers, and textures that trick your brain into craving more.

These foods stimulate a powerful dopamine response that overrides your normal satiety signals, leading to overconsumption. The processed food and fast-food industries, armed with vast marketing budgets, exploit your brain chemistry and emotions to create lifelong consumers. This combination of biological manipulation and relentless marketing has contributed to a global health crisis, with rising rates of obesity, diabetes, and heart disease linked directly to the consumption of ultra-processed foods.

It wasn't until some years later I could finally see the correlation in my own declining health; at my most overweight, battling multiple ongoing physical and mental health conditions, on a concoction of highly addictive prescription medications whilst also being fuelled by highly addictive ultra-processed foods.

Breaking the cycle of addiction to these foods requires awareness, re-education, and a commitment to choosing whole, minimally processed foods first. The food industry's immense financial power and sophisticated marketing strategies will continue to present a formidable challenge in the battle for long-term health and well-being.

However, by becoming aware of this mindset and making conscious changes, you can begin to shift your focus away from instant gratification and toward long-term well-being. Whether it's through building healthier habits, delaying gratification, or focusing on what truly matters, you do have the power to break free from the cycle of short-term pleasure and create a life that is truly fulfilling on the inside.

As I have learned from my journey, the path to long-term happiness is not always easy, but it is far more rewarding than any quick fix. I never thought I would say those words as someone who overconsumed daily.

True fulfillment comes from the journey itself—from the effort, persistence, and patience it takes to achieve meaningful goals. In a world that constantly encourages seeking instant gratification, the ability to delay pleasure in the pursuit of something greater may just be the key to lasting happiness.

Breaking cycles, particularly those related to instant gratification, unhealthy habits, or negative behaviours, can be challenging but transformative. Whether it's overeating, excessive consumption of material goods, procrastination, or other short-term fixes that provide temporary pleasure, breaking these cycles requires awareness, intention, and persistence. I've created a step-by-step guide to help you break these cycles and build healthier, more sustainable habits:

The first step in breaking any cycle is becoming aware of it.

Many habits are automatic, and we often don't even realise when we're engaging in them. Start by identifying your triggers, behaviours, and consequences of the cycle you want to break.

Track your habits: Keep a journal to log when, where, and why you engage in certain behaviours. For example, if you're trying to break a cycle of overeating, note when you overeat, what you eat, and how you feel before and after.

Identify emotional triggers: Instant gratification often occurs as a way to soothe negative emotions like stress, boredom, anxiety, or loneliness. Understanding your emotional triggers will help you manage them more effectively.

For example, I recognised in myself that stress and loneliness at the time were both major triggers for my unhealthy food cravings and alcohol consumption. By becoming aware of these emotional states, I could anticipate when I was vulnerable to falling into these habits.

You can't just break a cycle; you need to replace the behaviour with a healthier behaviour. Your brain thrives on routines and rewards, so you must provide an alternative that can satisfy the same emotional need without perpetuating the unhealthy habit.

Find healthier substitutes: If you're overeating to manage stress, find another way to release stress, like taking a walk, meditating, or engaging in a hobby you enjoy. If you're shopping to feel better emotionally, consider rewarding yourself with experiences rather than material items.

Gradual shifts: If a habit is deeply ingrained, start by making small changes. For example, if you're used to snacking on junk food every night, replace it with a healthier snack a few nights a week, gradually increasing the healthier days.

I found that swapping ultra-processed foods with fruit and yogurt allowed me to enjoy snacking without guilt or negative consequences. Similarly, I started doing quick mindfulness exercises when I felt the impulse to indulge.

Our 'have it now' culture has conditioned us to expect immediate rewards, but learning to delay gratification is a powerful tool in breaking cycles of instant pleasure. When you feel the urge to engage in habitual behaviour, consciously delay it.

Pause and reflect: Before indulging in a behaviour, take a moment to pause. Ask yourself if this action aligns with your long-term goals. For example, if you're about to order fast food, pause for five minutes, reflect on how you'll likely feel afterward, and then make a conscious choice based on that.

Set small time goals: If delaying gratification seems overwhelming, start with small steps. If you're used to making impulsive purchases, delay the purchase by twenty-four hours. If you're craving junk food, delay eating it for ten minutes. Often, by the time the delay is over, the urge to have it will have diminished.

Mindful rewards: Learn to associate longer-term rewards with satisfaction. For instance, if you're working on weight loss, celebrate weekly or monthly milestones rather than focusing on immediate results.

To truly break a cycle, you need to create new, positive habits that reinforce the change you're striving for. Habits are powerful because they become automatic, so developing ones that support your goals is crucial and will prevent the need for motivation and willpower.

Set realistic goals: Whether it's in your health, fitness, or any other area, make sure your goals are specific, achievable, and measurable. Small, realistic goals are more likely to create lasting change. For example, instead of saying, "I'll never eat junk food again," start with, "I will eat food that fuels my body and still allow myself to have and enjoy foods that I know are less nourishing from time to time."

Consistency over intensity: New habits stick when they're consistent. Even if the action feels small, doing it regularly matters more than doing it perfectly. For instance, committing to walking for ten minutes every day will have more impact than running for an hour once a week.

Reward progress: Reinforce new habits by acknowledging your progress. Even small successes should be celebrated. This could mean treating yourself to a new book after maintaining a week of mindful eating or taking time off after completing a significant fitness goal.

Breaking cycles will require a shift in mindset — from focusing on immediate rewards to prioritising long-term well-being. It's about adopting a perspective that values growth, patience, and long-term happiness.

Reframe your thinking: Instead of viewing short-term gratification as a reward, reframe it as something that delays your long-term success. Remind yourself that while the dopamine hit from instant gratification feels good at the moment, it can keep you from reaching your larger goals.

Visualise your future self: When you're tempted to fall back into old habits, think about your future self. How will you feel if you continue on your current path? Visualisation can be a powerful tool to motivate you to make healthier choices.

Focus on intrinsic rewards: Many of the behaviours we engage in for instant gratification are driven by external rewards, like looking good or getting approval from others. Instead, try to focus on intrinsic rewards, such as how good you feel when you take care of your body, the pride you experience from achieving a goal, or the personal satisfaction that comes from living in alignment with your values.

When I stopped seeking the immediate pleasure of food, I started focusing on how good I felt after making healthier choices. I began to value the internal rewards—feeling energised, confident, and at peace—more than the temporary pleasure of overindulging.

Breaking cycles is easier when you have the support and accountability of others on a similar path. Surround yourself with people who encourage your growth and help keep you on track.

I have something to add here. It may be an unpopular view, but I promised you from the beginning that I would be honest with you. On reflection, I know this has impacted my achievement of my goals for many years.

Not everyone will be a support when it comes to achieving your goals. Loved ones and friends may unconsciously try to persuade you away from them with well-meaning but unhelpful comments like "Come on, it's only one glass of wine" or "Surely one piece of cake won't hurt."

Find a coach: Having an expert to share your goals and progress with can help keep you on the right track. They can check in with you, offer encouragement, and provide expert strategies and guidance when you feel like slipping back into old habits.

Join a community: If you're trying to break a cycle related to health, weight loss, or personal growth, consider joining a group of like-minded individuals. Online communities, fitness groups, or local support groups can provide a sense of belonging, support, and accountability.

Share your journey: By sharing your goals and progress with others, you create a sense of responsibility for your actions. This could be through social media, a blog, or a personal journal. It's not about seeking validation but rather about creating accountability and reflecting on your growth.

Finally, it's important to recognise that breaking cycles is not easy, and setbacks are a completely normal part of the process. You may slip up from time to time, but that doesn't mean you've failed.

Self-compassion is key to staying on track and ultimately to achieving your goals.

Acknowledge setbacks: Instead of beating yourself up when you slip back into old habits, acknowledge what happened without judgment. Reflect on the trigger that caused the behaviour and consider what you can do differently next time.

Practice self-forgiveness: Understand that change takes time, and nobody is perfect. Forgive yourself for any mistakes, and focus on the progress you've made rather than the times you've fallen short. Treat yourself with kindness, as you would treat a friend who is going through the same struggle.

Use setbacks as learning opportunities: Rather than viewing setbacks as failures, see them as opportunities to learn more about yourself and your triggers. Each time you face a setback, you're gaining valuable insight into how to improve and move forward.

Breaking cycles of instant gratification and negative habits is challenging, but it's also one of the most rewarding things you can do for yourself. By understanding yourself and the patterns, replacing unhealthy behaviours with positive ones, practicing patience, and shifting your mindset, you can free yourself from the short-term pleasures that often hold you back.

For me, it took time to understand that my cravings for unhealthy food and alcohol were deep-rooted in a desire for instant gratification. By learning to delay these impulses and focus on long-term well-being, I was able to create new, healthier habits that have provided lasting happiness and fulfillment.

Remember, breaking cycles isn't about perfection; it's about progress. Each small step you take toward healthier habits and a more mindful approach to life brings you closer to the long-term happiness and fulfillment you deserve. With patience, persistence, and self-compassion, you can break free from the cycle and build a life that aligns with your deepest values and goals.

Breaking cycles, particularly those rooted in instant gratification, requires intentional action, patience, and self-awareness. I know it can feel overwhelming at first, especially if your habits are deeply ingrained, but by taking small, manageable steps, you can begin to create meaningful change in your life.

Here's how you can get started:

Before you can break a cycle, you need to clearly understand what it is. Start by reflecting on areas of your life where you feel stuck or unsatisfied. Where do you consistently turn to instant gratification, even if it's harmful in the long run? This could involve:

- Unhealthy eating habits
- Excessive alcohol or junk food consumption
- Procrastination or avoidance of important tasks
- Dependency on social media for validation or entertainment

Action step: Write down one or two specific habits or behaviours that are part of a larger cycle you want to break. Be as specific as possible. For example, instead of just saying, "I want to stop overeating," you might write, "I want to stop turning to junk food when I'm stressed after work," or "I want to stop turning to alcohol to give me confidence."

Understand Your Triggers

To start breaking a cycle, it's essential to understand what triggers your behaviour. Triggers can be emotional (e.g., stress, boredom, loneliness), environmental (e.g., time of day, certain places), or social (e.g., peer pressure, being around certain people). These triggers prompt your brain to seek out a dopamine hit through unhealthy behaviours.

Action step: Over the next few days, track when you engage in the habit you're trying to change. Write down what was happening right before you did it — what were you feeling, thinking, or experiencing? This will help you recognise patterns and anticipate moments when you're vulnerable.

Set Clear, Realistic Goals

When breaking cycles, it's important to set small, achievable goals rather than overwhelm yourself with unrealistic expectations. Aiming to completely overhaul your habits overnight often leads to frustration and setbacks.

Start small: Focus on one habit at a time. For example, if you want to reduce your unhealthy eating, start by reducing the amount of ultra-processed food you eat at one meal each day rather than trying to eliminate it.

Make goals measurable: Create specific and measurable goals so you can track your progress. Instead of saying, "I want to eat healthier," say, "I will eat a homemade lunch instead of buying fast food at least three times this week."

Action step: Set one small, specific goal related to the habit or cycle you want to break. Write it down and commit to it for the next week. This could be as simple as delaying ordering a takeaway by ten minutes or committing to a ten-minute walk after dinner instead of sitting down to watch TV and reaching for snacks.

Create an Action Plan

Once you know your triggers and have set a clear goal, develop a plan to change your behaviour. Think about how you can avoid triggers or create new, healthier responses when faced with them.

Change your environment: If your environment makes it easy to fall back into old habits, change it. For example, if you find yourself overeating at night, don't keep tempting snacks in the house, or if you always open a bottle of wine from the fridge at the end of the week, remove the wine from the fridge.

Find healthy replacements: Replace your unhealthy habits with healthier alternatives. If you typically grab junk food when you're stressed, try preparing healthier snacks in advance or reach for fruit instead of ultra-processed snacks.

Prepare for discomfort: Changes in habits will likely feel uncomfortable at first. Acknowledge that it's normal to experience cravings or resistance, but remind yourself why you're making these changes and how they will benefit you in the long term.

Action step: Write down your action plan, including what you'll do when you're triggered and how you'll replace your old habit with a new one. For example, if stress at work leads to emotional eating, you might plan to take a five-minute walk instead of reaching for food.

Practice Delayed Gratification

Learning to delay gratification is crucial when trying to break cycles of instant pleasure. It helps to break the automatic response that leads to short-term fixes. Contrary to popular belief you don't have to completely deny yourself the things you enjoy, but practice delaying the impulse to seek them immediately.

Use the Ten-minute rule: When you feel the urge to indulge in an unhealthy habit, delay the action by ten minutes. During that time, distract yourself with another activity (e.g., take a walk, drink water, or call a friend). Often, the urge will pass by the time the ten minutes are up.

Build up gradually: Start by delaying gratification for small things and work your way up to bigger challenges.

Action step: The next time you feel the urge to engage in your habit (whether it's overeating, ordering a take-away, or something else), pause for ten minutes. During that time, think about how you'll feel afterward if you indulge versus how you'll feel if you don't.

Track Your Progress and Celebrate Wins

Tracking your progress helps you stay motivated and allows you to see the changes you're making over time. It's important to acknowledge small victories, even if they feel minor.

Keep a journal or log: Write down your goals, triggers, and progress daily or weekly. Reflect on what went well and where you may have found it more challenging. This can help you identify patterns and make adjustments as needed.

Celebrate small wins: Recognise and reward yourself for progress, no matter how small. If you successfully avoid emotional eating for a week, treat yourself to a non-food reward, such as a massage, a new book, or time spent on a hobby you enjoy.

Action step: Start a journal or digital log where you can track your progress. Include your goals, the actions you took to resist these temptations, and how you felt after making healthier choices. Each week, review your progress and celebrate your wins.

Build a Support System

Breaking cycles is easier when you have people to support you and hold you accountable. Whether it's a coach or a community group, having someone to share your journey with can motivate and encourage you.

Share your goals: Tell someone you trust and also support your desire to achieve your goals about the cycle you're trying to break. This adds a layer of accountability and makes it harder to slip back into old habits unnoticed.

Seek support from like-minded people: Join a group or community where others are working toward similar goals. Knowing that others are going through the same struggles and challenges can be incredibly motivating, especially when there is no fear of judgment, shame, or embarrassment.

Action step: Identify one person or group with whom you can share your goal. Tell them what you're working on and ask if they'd be willing to check in with you regularly to help keep you on track.

Be Kind to Yourself: Practice Self-Compassion

Breaking cycles takes time, and setbacks are inevitable. The key is not to give up when you slip but to practice self-compassion and get back on track. Criticising yourself when you make mistakes, as I found to be true, can lead to a cycle of guilt and shame, making it harder to continue.

Acknowledge setbacks without judgment: If you fall back into old habits, which will inevitably happen from time to time, don't beat yourself up. Acknowledge what happened, reflect on what triggered the behaviour, and decide what you can do differently next time.

Focus on progress, not perfection: Remember that breaking cycles is about progress, not perfection. Every step in the right direction is a success, no matter how small it may seem at the time.

Action step: If you experience a setback, take a moment to reflect on it with kindness. Write down what triggered the behaviour, what you learned from it, and what you'll do differently moving forward. Remind yourself that change is a process, and if you've started, then you're already on the right path.

By taking these steps, you'll strengthen your foundation for breaking unhealthy cycles and building lasting, positive habits. Each small change adds up, and over time, you'll feel more in control and aligned with your long-term goals.

Chapter Three

Changing Your Story - A Journey from Self-Limitation to Empowerment

"Maybe the journey isn't so much about becoming anything. Maybe it's about un-becoming everything that isn't really you so you can be who you were meant to be in the first place"

– Paulo Coelho

This has quickly become one of my favourite quotes, and I feel it accurately sums up my personal weight loss, health, and life transformation journey. However, I could never quite put my finger on it. I always felt something was amiss in my life. I felt like a square peg in a round hole, so to speak, until I discovered what I now refer to as the unbecoming process of letting go of all the literal and metaphorical weight I had been holding onto and carrying throughout my life.

I want you to know that changing your story is not only highly possible but also entirely within your control, no matter how fixed or unchangeable your narrative may seem at present.

We are all conditioned by our environment, our upbringing, and our experiences, and as I have discovered, these factors deeply influence our beliefs about ourselves.

For much of my life, I held onto labels and beliefs that restricted me and shaped a story filled with hardship, struggle, pain, and self-limitation. I was constantly battling with my weight, consumed by emotional eating, suffering from chronic pain, constant illness, fatigue, depression, anxiety, and low self-esteem. My mindset was rigid, and my self-worth was fragile at best.

I had an innate tendency to give up when things got difficult or didn't go according to plan. I always waited for the illusion of the 'perfect' moment and repeatedly sabotaged my progress in many areas of my life.

But I am here as living proof that it is possible to rewrite your story, break free from the chains of limiting beliefs, and create a life full of health, vitality, genuine confidence, and joy.

In this chapter, I will share my personal journey of transformation—how I went from a woman weighed down by her physical weight, chronic pain, emotional struggles, and self-doubt to someone who is now the healthiest, happiest, and most resilient version of myself.

I will also explore and explain in more detail why you may be finding it difficult to make the long-term changes you want to with your weight and health, despite a deep desire to do so, and how understanding the very nature of your thoughts and beliefs will *ultimately* give you the freedom you desire.

Before delving into my own personal transformation, I feel it is important for me to explain how your brain works, particularly when it comes to thought patterns and beliefs. I had no understanding of this until I commenced my own research in 2019. If this *was* taught at school, which I highly doubt it was, I think it's safe to say I missed the whole syllabus due to another bout of illness!

Research suggests that, on average, we have between **60,000 and 70,000 thoughts daily,** and a staggering **90-95% of these thoughts are repetitive.**

In short, this means that most of what you think about today is the same as what you thought about yesterday and the day before that.

So, if you have been struggling with self-doubt, anxiety, or negative self-talk for some time, know that these thoughts are most likely repeating over and over, reinforcing themselves like a loop, a broken and stuck record.

Your brain is hard-wired for efficiency, meaning it prefers to rely on familiar patterns. This is why changing your thoughts and beliefs can feel so difficult. Maybe you feel that after so many failed attempts, it is an impossible task.

When a belief or thought is repeated often enough, it becomes ingrained in your neural pathways, much like a well-trodden path in the woods. This is particularly true for the stories you repeatedly tell yourself about who you are.

If you constantly think, "I'm not good enough," "I'll never be healthy," or "I'm an emotional eater," your brain will accept all of those statements as facts.

I know it seems counterproductive and even unfair that your brain has been wired in this way.

I felt the same until I learned the strategies to reprogram it.

Unfortunately, as much as you may consciously want to change, wanting is not enough. These deeply embedded beliefs will continuously pull you back into your old habits and behaviour patterns unless you learn how to challenge and replace them.

Your upbringing and early experiences will play a crucial role in forming these beliefs. Many of us, including myself, have been given limiting beliefs by others that, over time, shape our self-perception and define the stories we eventually live by.

In my case, these beliefs, which I turned into self-addressed labels, not only hindered my growth and my physical and mental health but also led me to a continuous cycle of self-sabotage, especially around food that, for most of my life, seemed impossible to break.

From a young age, I was labeled as a "poorly child." Born with whooping cough and already with a weakened immune system, I was constantly falling ill as a child; this led to long periods of absence from school and feeling deeply disconnected from my peers.

Well-meaning family members, medical professionals, and teachers reinforced this label, often reminding me of how "fragile" and "weak" I was.

I vividly remember in junior school, one teacher 'affectionately' referred to me as a 'Woolworths baby,' making reference to the fact I was made of poor quality and there was a clear defect with me; this was repeated to me each time I returned to school after yet another period of absenteeism.

Over time, I internalised this identity as that of someone who was always weaker than others. I struggled continuously with my schoolwork, which was hardly surprising considering the large gaps in my education due to consistent absences from school. This led to frequent tellings by some teachers that my performance was below average, including one teacher who said when I was eight years old that my schoolwork was evidence that I would "never amount to anything."

These messages played out in my mind repeatedly and stuck with me, I left school, as expected, with well below average GCSE results, limiting me with the choices this afforded me for my further education, and in turn, my career opportunities only reinforced this belief. These beliefs became a part of my story and, ultimately, an even bigger part of my identity for many years.

At the time, I had no idea or concept that the beliefs I had grown up with weren't set in stone. I had accepted them to be true, and because of that, I never challenged myself to see who I truly could be. I carried these beliefs and self-addressed labels well into adulthood, where they played a significant role in shaping my self-esteem, confidence, and, ultimately, my health and happiness. Whilst I tried hard at everything I did, I was convinced that I was limited by my life circumstances—by my physical health, by my lack of academic success, and by the emotional struggles that I had experienced for so many years.

These beliefs laid the foundation for my later battles with emotional eating, chronic pain, depression, and anxiety. I felt powerless to change because I had accepted that this was just simply 'who I was'—a sick, unworthy person who wasn't good enough to succeed or have an abundance of good health and fortune.

Before I was sixteen, my life took a devastating and unexpected turn.

My mum, who had always been my anchor and guiding light, suffered a tragic decline in her health that changed everything.

She had already been battling with a chronic illness for four years—an illness that had deeply impacted every area of her health and had forced her to give up her cherished career and lifelong vocation as a nurse, a profession she had loved deeply and one everyone said she was born for.

Despite her health battles, my mum remained a source of comfort and strength to me during mine. I looked up to her in every way, and our bond was something I treasured. She was my role model, and I had always felt incredibly close to her.

But shortly before my sixteenth birthday, when my Mum was just forty-nine, everything dramatically changed. My mum was prescribed a benzodiazepine in an attempt to manage her deteriorating condition and to help calm her nervous system, but instead of helping, the medication had catastrophic effects and caused irreparable damage to her brain.

The mother I knew and loved was suddenly gone, not physically, but mentally and emotionally. The damage was so severe that for the last three years of her life, she was too ill to have contact with me.

She remained bedridden until she passed away from multiple organ failure on 19th July 1994.

This was an incredibly painful and isolating time for me. I was still a teenager, already trying to navigate the ups and downs of adolescence, finding my education a continuous challenge to navigate, and now I had to face the heartbreaking reality of losing my mum in a way that

felt both gradual and yet so overwhelming simultane-
ously. She had been such a central figure in my life, and
suddenly, I found myself without her guidance, her love,
and her presence.

Even though I had a loving family and friends, the loss
of my mum at that age felt like a deep and personal
rejection. I felt abandoned, as if the one person who had
truly understood me had been taken away. Her illness
and eventual death left a void in my life that no one else
could fill. I struggled to make sense of why this had
happened, and for over two and a half decades, I carried
the weight of this loss and burden with me. The feelings of rejection and abandonment were always there,
lingering in the background, and they had a profound
effect on my self-worth, my confidence, and even my
relationships.

In many ways, I felt that if my mum, the person who had
loved me unconditionally from birth, could no longer
be there for me, then maybe I wasn't worthy of love or
affection from others. I began to internalise this sense
of rejection, and it coloured how I saw myself and how
I interacted with the world. It reinforced all the negative
beliefs I already held about myself—that I wasn't good
enough, that I was somehow flawed or unlovable.

For nearly twenty-five years, this loss impacted me in
ways I couldn't fully understand at the time. It mani-
fested in my relationships, where I often struggled with
insecurity, a fear of abandonment, and a reluctance
to fully trust others. Even though I was surrounded
by people who I knew deeply cared about me, the

emotional wound from losing my mum left me feeling isolated and disconnected.

It was a time that I noticeably increased my use of food and alcohol as a coping mechanism to soothe emotions and feelings that I simply didn't have the understanding or the tools to navigate.

Food had been, for as long as I could recall, a love language in our family.

Some of my earliest memories in our first family home were the time my Mum made me a plate of cheese on toast as she lovingly attended to my badly cut knee after I carelessly tobogganed under a neighbour's static car on the icy road outside our house and sitting down to watch the Grand National with a vast spread of food, what she liked to call a 'picky tea'.

When she wasn't working, she was always in the kitchen baking and cooking for her own family and others.

Homemade treats galore were stored in Tupperware containers: macaroons, flapjacks, sausage rolls, and cheese scones.

During my Mum's illness and for a while after she died, a constant delivery of homemade food parcels would turn up at our back door. Food, yet again, represented love in my eyes, but this time, a loss of the love I so desperately craved and needed at this point in my life.

I used what I knew best to replace the loss of love from my Mum.

Food.

It wasn't until much later in life, in my early forties, when I began the process of healing and deeper transformation that I started to confront the deep-seated impact of this loss. I realised that feelings of rejection, shame, and abandonment were at the core of my struggles with self-worth and confidence. Finally, being able to name and understand these feelings was a critical part of the journey toward rewriting my own story.

Though looking back this chapter of my life was filled with immense pain and sorrow, it also played a pivotal role in shaping who I have become today. After years of avoidance, it finally enabled me to confront the most difficult emotions I had ever experienced, and ultimately, it became a great source of strength. Through this deep loss, I learned the importance of resilience and the power of self-compassion. I came to understand and accept that while my mum's illness and her death was a heartbreaking tragedy, it didn't define me. I could still honour her memory while also reclaiming my own life, my own story.

In the years that followed, I gradually found the courage to heal from the pain of losing my mum. It wasn't an easy process, and it took time, but it was through this healing that I began to rebuild my sense of self-worth, another poignant part of my weight loss journey.

I learned that I am truly deserving of love, not because of what others think or how they treat me, but because of who I am. That starts with my own love. It's been a long journey, but one that ultimately brought me to a place of peace, acceptance, and self-love.

Today, as I reflect on this journey, I can now see how my mum's illness and her untimely death shaped so many aspects of my life. But I also see how I have grown from that experience, how it has eventually made me stronger and more compassionate toward myself and others.

For too many years, I allowed myself to become a victim of these circumstances. I always looked outward to pass the blame for my behaviours and, ultimately, my life until I finally realised that I was both the problem and the solution.

While I still carry the memory of that loss with me, I now know that it doesn't have to define my future.

I had the power to change my story, to get on the path to live a life filled with health, happiness, and fulfillment. In doing so, I honour not only myself but also the memory of my mum, who always believed in me, even when I struggled to believe in myself.

Though marked by deep pain, this part of my story has ultimately been a significant source of transformation. It has taught me that even in the face of the most difficult challenges, you have the power to rewrite your narratives and create a life that reflects your true potential.

One of the most significant struggles I faced during this period of my life was with my weight. Like many people, I used food as a way to cope with stress, sadness, and frustration. Emotional eating became a crutch, and I felt helpless to control it. I would go through cycles of dieting and then bingeing, punishing myself with guilt and shame after every setback. Each time I tried to lose weight or improve my health, I found an excuse to give up. My fixed mindset told me that I was simply not capable of changing. I believed that I was destined to struggle with my weight and that emotional eating was something I would never overcome.

The emotional pain I carried only deepened these struggles.

I was battling chronic pain and illness daily, which seemed to confirm the belief that I was a "sickly" person who would never be truly healthy. My physical discomfort fed into the depression and anxiety I already battled, and vice versa. It was a vicious cycle, and I didn't know how to break free.

I suffered from extremely low self-esteem. Constantly comparing myself to others and feelings of inadequacy in every area of my life. I saw others achieving things I believed I could never accomplish, whether it was related to their health, career, or relationships.

I was stuck in a story that I believed was unchangeable, and the thought of rewriting it felt impossible.

The turning point in my journey came when I hit a rock-bottom moment.

To be clear, there have been many more than one.

I realised that I was not living the life I wanted, and I had become sick and tired of feeling like a victim of my circumstances. This moment of clarity came not from a single event but from a gradual accumulation of frustration and self-reflection. I had spent years blaming external factors—my grief, my health, my lack of oppor-tunities, my lack of time—but I began to see that while these things may have influenced my story, they didn't have to define it.

I started to ask myself: *What if the beliefs I've held about myself all these years aren't actually true? What if I'm capable of more than I think?*

This shift in mindset was small at first, but it planted the seed for a much deeper transformation.

One of the most powerful lessons I learned during this time was that **the labels and beliefs we attach to ourselves are not permanent.**

Just because I had been told I was a "sickly child" didn't mean I had to live my entire life as a sick person. Just because I had struggled with school didn't mean I was unintelligent or incapable of having success. These were stories I had been telling myself repeatedly for years, and it was time to finally challenge them.

The first step in my transformation was becoming aware of my inner dialogue. In case you need reassurance, those constant voices in your head you hear? You're not going mad as I thought I was for many years. They are completely normal.

I started to pay attention to my thoughts each day—thoughts like, "I'll never be healthy," "I'm not good enough," or "I always fail at everything I try."

I acknowledged that these thoughts were not only untrue but also kept me stuck in the same patterns of unhelpful

& destructive behaviour. If I believed I would always fail, then, of course, I would continue to give up at the first hurdle. If I believed I wasn't good enough, then, unsurprisingly, I would never have the confidence or desire to pursue my goals.

I began to consciously challenge these thoughts. Instead of accepting them as fact, I asked myself, *What if the opposite is true? What if I am capable of being healthy and strong? What if I can live a pain-free life? What if I am good enough to achieve my goals? What if I can break free from emotional eating and take control of my life?* These questions opened up new possibilities that I had never previously considered.

In addition to challenging my thoughts, I started practicing positive affirmations. This may sound simple, but it was incredibly powerful for me at the beginning of my transformation journey. Every day, I repeated affirmations like "I am healthy," "I am worthy," and "I am capable of change." Over time, these affirmations began to replace the negative thoughts and voices that had been dominating my mind for so long.

One of the greatest shifts I experienced during this process was breaking free from the ties of emotional eating. For as long as I can remember, I have turned to food as a source of comfort, using it to numb difficult emotions that I didn't want to confront.

This behaviour stemmed from an early age. I remember when school felt overwhelming and all-consuming, I would spend all my pocket money in the school tuck shop or at the general convenience store down the road on crisps, sweets, and chocolate bars. The moment I consumed them, I felt a little calmer, a temporary soothing of all the negative emotions I was experiencing at that moment, however short-lived they were.

When my mum passed away, that love language changed dramatically.

The kitchen, once the heart and soul of our home, became a quieter, emptier place. I found myself navigating not only the grief of losing her but also the physical void she left in our household. Without her, it felt like a significant part of my emotional foundation had crumbled.

In the wake of her death, food once again took up a source of great emotional comfort to me, but in a very different way.

Instead of lovingly prepared meals or thoughtful notes, I turned to a simpler, more convenient way of eating: convenience food. The go-to became the local fish and chip shop. There was something about the ritual of heading to the chippy after an emotionally tiring day that offered a sense of routine, a way to ground myself amid overwhelming grief. It wasn't about the food itself—it was greasy, salty, and far from the healthiest choice—but it was about the comfort it provided and the memories it brought back.

On my way home from the fish and chip shop, I'd make a detour to the local off-license, where I'd buy multiple chocolate bars. This tradition began after my mum's death and helped me cope in its own way.

This routine wasn't just about food—it was about filling a deep void. In those moments, I felt comforted in my grief, where I didn't have the words to express it. Food became a friend and, most importantly, one who didn't judge me. The fish and chips, the chocolate bars—they were a way to soothe the emptiness, to find comfort in something familiar when everything else felt so uncertain.

Food has long been a symbol of celebration across many cultures, and my family was no different. While food comforted us in times of loss, it was also central to the happiest moments of our lives.

In our household, every holiday and special occasion was marked by a feast. I can remember my Mother shopping and baking for holidays months in advance. Christmas was a time when the kitchen was alive with the smell of meat, roast potatoes, and all the trimmings. Easter brought with it the tradition of baking hot cross buns and indulging in far too many chocolate eggs. Birthdays, too, were celebrated with thoughtful homemade cakes, each one baked with love and decorated to perfection by my mother.

These celebrations were moments when food brought us all together. It was never just about the eating—it was about the process of preparing the food, the excitement of gathering around the table, and the shared experience of indulging in something delicious. Food marked the significance of the occasion, elevating the celebration and making it feel more special.

Even beyond traditional holidays, food was a part of celebrating the small wins in life. When someone got a good grade or achieved something at school or work, there was always a treat waiting to mark the occasion. I remember the end-of-school-year treat, always a family visit to the local Wimpy restaurant for a cheeseburger and chips followed by the legendary Brown Derby!

Food was intertwined with joy, accomplishment, and togetherness. It was how we expressed our happiness and pride in one another as a family.

Just as food was central to celebration, it also played a significant role in how we dealt with loss, sadness, and difficult times. It's a phenomenon that stretches far beyond my own experience—across cultures and throughout history, food has been a way to commemorate the loss of loved ones or to provide comfort in times of difficulty.

When someone passes away, it's common for food to be brought to the family of the deceased. It's a way for the community to show support, to say, "We are here for you." The act of cooking and sharing food in these moments becomes a form of emotional support, a way to nourish the body when the heart is heavy with grief.

After my mum's death, friends and family members would bring over casseroles, cakes, and other dishes, filling our kitchen with food we hadn't asked for but appreciated deeply. In those moments, the food was more than sustenance—it was a lifeline. It was a way for people to offer their love and support when words often fell short.

In some ways, this tradition of using food as comfort became a part of my emotional coping mechanisms. Whenever life became too much—whether it was stress from work, personal struggles in my relationships, or the lingering sadness of loss—I would find myself turning to food and alcohol for comfort.

It wasn't always a conscious decision, but it became a pattern of my behaviour. Just as fish and chips had been a source of comfort after my mum's death, other foods became associated with my emotional relief. Chocolate, ice cream, or even a big bowl of pasta would momentarily soothe whatever difficult emotion I was dealing with at that time.

My relationship with food has evolved and expanded over the years. What started as a love language, a way for my mother to show her deep care and affection, became something more complex as I navigated the highs and lows of life. Food, for me, became intertwined with emotion in a way that, all too often, wasn't healthy. While it brought comfort in times of sadness and celebration in moments of joy, it also became a way for me to numb the emotions that I ultimately didn't want to deal with or, maybe more importantly, didn't know how to.

Many people, including many of my clients, experience emotional eating. It's the tendency to turn to food not out of hunger but to cope with emotions such as stress, sadness, loneliness, or even boredom.

In many ways, emotional eating can provide temporary relief. Eating something sweet or indulgent triggers the release of feel-good hormones, offering a brief moment of comfort. But the downside is that the comfort initially experienced is often fleeting, and when repeated frequently it can lead to an unhealthy relationship with food and your body.

For me, recognising this pattern has been an important step in understanding my emotional landscape.

It has made me more aware of how I used food and alcohol to cope and, in turn, has allowed me to explore healthier ways of dealing with my emotions. This doesn't mean that I no longer find comfort in food—there will always be a part of me that associates a warm meal or a sweet dessert with love and care. But I have since learned to strike a healthier balance, to enjoy food for what it is, without letting it become the sole way of navigating my emotions.

My personal story with food is just one of countless examples of how food plays a significant role in our emotional lives. Across the world, food is used to celebrate, to comfort, and to connect people. Whether it's a family gathering around the table for a holiday meal, a couple sharing a romantic dinner, or friends offering casseroles in times of grief, food is a universal language that transcends words.

In many cultures, food is used as a way to honour religious and cultural traditions. During Christmas, for example, families gather to share a festive meal, marking the holiday with specific dishes that have been passed down through generations. Easter often brings with it its culinary traditions, from chocolate eggs to roast lamb. For those who celebrate alternative religious holidays—such as Diwali, Ramadan, or Hanukkah—food plays an equally important role. It is a way to bring people together, to celebrate faith and tradition, and to mark the passage of time.

Even outside of religious celebrations, food commemorates important life events. Weddings are often celebrated with elaborate feasts, while birthdays are marked with cakes and sweets. Funerals, too, are occasions where food is used to bring people together and offer comfort in the face of loss. I vividly remember, as a teenager, making and cutting enough sandwiches to feed an army on the day of my own Mum's funeral to ensure no one went hungry at the wake we hosted for her in our back garden.

In these moments, food becomes more than just something to eat—it becomes a symbol of connection, of care, of love.

Food has always been a constant presence in my life, shaping my emotions, memories, and relationships. From my mother's lovingly prepared meals and treats to the fish and chips and chocolate bars I would eat after her death, food has always been more than just sustenance. It has been a love language, a way to celebrate, and a source of comfort in times of grief.

My journey with food has also taught me about the complexity of emotional eating. While food can offer comfort and connection, it can also become a way to avoid dealing with difficult emotions. Understanding this has been an important part of my personal growth.

Ultimately, food will always be a part of our emotional lives. Whether we celebrate, comfort, or connect with it, it remains one of the most powerful ways we express love and care for ourselves and others.

But as I worked on changing my mindset and beliefs around food, I realised that emotional eating was just another symptom of the deeper issue—my belief that I wasn't good enough or capable of change.

I began to develop healthier coping mechanisms for dealing with stress and emotions. Instead of reaching for food, I started journaling, meditating, and engaging in physical activity. I also learned to recognise when I was eating out of emotion rather than hunger, and I developed strategies to interrupt the cycle. By addressing the root cause of my emotional eating—my negative self-beliefs—I was able to regain control of my relationship with food.

One of the most unexpected yet rewarding aspects of my transformation has been the development of resilience and mental strength. In the past, I would give up as soon as I encountered a challenge or setback. But as I worked on changing my mindset around my weight and emotional eating, I started to see challenges in other areas of my life as opportunities for growth rather than as reasons to quit.

I adopted a **growth mindset**, which is the belief that our abilities and emotional intelligence can be developed through effort and perseverance. This was a major shift for me, as I had always believed that my circumstances inherently limited me. With a growth mindset, I began to approach challenges and setbacks with curiosity and determination rather than fear and self-doubt, as I had done previously.

Each time I faced a hurdle—whether related to my health, my business, or challenges in my personal life—I reminded myself that setbacks are a natural part of growth. Instead of giving up, I learned to navigate through, knowing that each challenge was, in some way, making me stronger.

Depression and anxiety have been constant companions for much of my life. From as early as fourteen, when I was struggling with the impact of my Mum's declining health and the constant difficulties with my health, I was referred for psychiatric assessment and treatment.

My mental health challenges were deeply intertwined with my low self-esteem and feelings of inadequacy, and I came to realise that I was also being impacted heavily by the choices I made with my food. But as I began to change my mindset, be more mindful of my eating, and rewrite my story, I found that my mental health started to improve vastly.

One of the key factors in overcoming depression and anxiety for me was learning to be kinder to myself.

For years, I had been my own worst critic, constantly beating myself up for not being "good enough." But as I started to challenge my negative thoughts and beliefs, I also learned to practice self-compassion. I finally realised that I didn't have to be perfect to be worthy of love and happiness.

I also started to focus on gratitude.

Each day, I made a point to acknowledge the things in my life that I was grateful for, no matter how small. This simple practice helped me to shift my focus away from what I felt I was at that time missing in my life and toward what I already had. Over time, this shift in perspective helped to lift the heavy cloud of depression and ease the constant worry of anxiety that had been a main feature throughout my childhood and adult life.

Today, I am the healthiest and most at peace I have ever been.

I have learned that y**our** *story is not set in stone—it can be rewritten* at any time. The key is to challenge the beliefs that are holding you back and replace them with empowering, positive ones.

By changing my mindset, I was able to break free from the cycle of emotional eating, overcome chronic pain, and take control of my physical health. I am now in the best shape of my life, physically, mentally, and emotionally. I have developed resilience, mental strength, and a deep sense of self-worth. I no longer see myself as a victim of my circumstances but as someone who is capable of creating the life I want.

If you're struggling with limiting beliefs, self-doubt, or a fixed mindset, know that it is entirely possible to change your story.

You don't have to be defined by the labels others have placed on you or by the beliefs you've held about yourself for years. The key is to become aware of your thoughts, to challenge the ones that are holding you back, and to replace them with empowering beliefs.

Changing your story is not easy, and it won't happen overnight. But with a little persistence, self-compassion, and a willingness to grow, you can break free from any patterns that have been keeping you stuck and create a life filled with health, happiness, and fulfilment.

What story have you told yourself up until now? The story that you're an emotional eater? The story that you'll always struggle with your weight? The story that this is just who you are?

Your story is entirely yours to write—so don't let anyone else hold the pen!

Maybe it's time for you to create a new story.

Chapter Four

No Is a Full Sentence: Reclaiming Yourself through Boundaries

"If you always do what you've always done, you'll always get what you've always got."

– Henry Ford, founder of the Ford Motor Company

Something I repeatedly told myself in my quest for long-term change was, 'I knew what I needed to do; I just needed to do it.' The truth, I can now freely admit, is that I actually didn't.

I knew only what I had previously known, but it soon became evident that this knowledge was not a successful strategy for making sustainable, long-term changes to my weight, my health, and, ultimately, my overall happiness in life.

I knew everything about diets, and I'd certainly done enough of them, but what I didn't know was how to create optimal physical, mental, and emotional well-being in synergy with a busy lifestyle and ever-increasing responsibilities.

Ultimately, I didn't know how to create inner fulfilment and happiness, as this was not a subject we were taught at school.

It's clear that we live in a world that often values compliance over conviction. In our constant desire to please others, we become conditioned to say "yes" when our hearts, minds, and bodies are often screaming "no."

This tendency to prioritise the needs of others over our own is not only a betrayal of our authentic selves, but it can also have devastating effects on our physical and emotional well-being, as I discovered only too well for myself.

In this chapter, we'll explore how saying "no" is not only a boundary but a form of self-respect and a key to reclaiming your life and your health. We'll also dive into how our inability to say "no" can often stem from childhood, societal expectations, your desire for validation, and how, in my case, it was fuelled by a response to the trauma I experienced in adolescence.

I'll share details of my journey, including how the loss of my mother shaped my need to please others as a form of self-validation and how this unhealthy dynamic played out in my relationships, my body, and my life for many years.

Most of us were 'trained,' from an early age to say "yes."

I was raised in a loving and respectful family, and from childhood, I was taught to be polite, agreeable, and accommodating. I was told to say no to strangers but be respectful and say yes to everyone else. In principle, these sound like strong ethics and values to live by until saying yes to everyone else consistently means saying no to yourself.

As a child, I had no idea what people-pleasing even was. Now, looking back on many of my childhood experiences, I know that when I went the extra mile and did things to make others happy, whether at home or at school, I received praise and validation, which seemed to give me a much-needed sense of worthiness.

My early struggles with health and academics left me feeling like I wasn't fulfilling my potential and that I was letting myself and others down. Looking back, I know I had a desperate desire to compensate for my shortcomings, and being a people-pleaser simply became part of my nature, one of my ingrained default settings, another habit.

Whether it is accepting food you don't want, taking on tasks you don't have the energy for, or attending social events out of a feeling of obligation, the result is sadly the same: you often end up betraying your own needs as a consequence.

The price you can pay for this people-pleasing mentality can be steep, often showing up in the form of burnout, stress, weight gain, resentment, and a deep sense of dissatisfaction with life.

Think about it for a moment.

How many times have you eaten a piece of cake at a family gathering or had another drink at a party, not because you wanted it, but because you felt you should say yes and any other response would appear rude? Or how often have you taken on extra responsibilities at work or for a friend, despite already feeling completely overwhelmed with your responsibilities, because you didn't want to let anyone down?

Every time you say yes to something that doesn't serve you, you're essentially saying no to yourself. While this may seem like nothing in the short term, the long-term impact can leave you feeling resentful at best and entirely burned out at worst.

This pattern of people-pleasing can also be incred-ibly detrimental to your health. When you don't have clear boundaries with yourself and others, you will likely struggle to say no to things that may be nega-tively affecting you, such as unhealthy food, excessive drinking, or staying up late. Over time, as I discovered, this continued behaviour can lead to weight gain, diges-tive issues, fatigue, and even chronic health conditions. The cake you didn't really want, the glass of wine you could have done without, the late-night dessert you ate out of guilt rather than hunger—each one represents a small betrayal of your own needs in favour of someone else's expectations.

Your body often bears the brunt of your inability to set and follow through on boundaries. When we constantly say "yes" to the wrong things—whether it's food, commitments, or relationships—we're putting unnecessary strain on our own physical well-being. For example, you might find it difficult to refuse dessert at a friend's house because you've been taught it's impolite to do so. But what happens when you repeatedly say yes to unhealthy food choices in all situations like this?

Over time, these small and seemingly less harmful decisions have a compounding effect and can lead to excessive weight gain, digestive issues, and even longer-term health conditions such as diabetes or high blood pressure.

In my own experience, I can recall numerous occasions where I found I lacked clear boundaries when eating something I didn't enjoy or want—simply because I didn't want to disappoint the person offering it or appear to be rude.

For years after my Mother passed away, my father would thoughtfully buy and proudly serve me stollen cake when I returned home each Christmas. I had never liked stollen cake; in fact, I detested it. Yet, every year, I would smile, eat multiple slices, and politely thank him for buying it.

Why? I didn't want to hurt his feelings by saying no, and I feared that one small refusal would make him feel rejected. At that moment and for subsequent years, I chose to put his feelings over my own needs, which resulted in my discomfort.

We joke about the stollen cake now after I finally owned up to my dislike of it, something I felt I wanted to do when I started to set clear boundaries and follow through on them.

The very fact we laugh about it shows that when boundaries are set and communicated effectively with people who truly care about you, no one gets hurt or stops loving you for it.

This story may seem somewhat trivial, but it exemplifies how easy it is to let others' desires and feelings control our actions, even when it comes to something as personal as what we eat and put in our bodies. There have been too many times to count when I accepted the piece of cake, another glass of wine, and a second helping of dinner because I didn't feel comfortable saying no.

Now, multiply this pattern across other aspects of your life, and you begin to see the full picture of how saying "yes" to others and "no" to yourself can slowly erode your sense of self.

People-pleasing takes a physical toll, as well as emotional and metaphorical weight. When you constantly strive to meet others' expectations, you often lose touch with your authentic self. You will most likely become a version of yourself shaped by the needs, desires, and demands of others rather than your true nature. You often feel like a chameleon, continuously adapting to every situation to ensure acceptance, love, and value.

For me, this dynamic became especially pronounced after the loss of my mother. Her passing left a deep void in my life, and in that void, I developed a desperate need to feel needed, loved, and valued by others.

I continuously sought validation through people-pleasing, believing that if I could keep everyone else happy, I might somehow fill the emptiness and loneliness I felt inside. I thought that by saying yes to everyone's needs, I would secure their approval and, in turn, feel worthy of the love and connection that I longed for.

This pattern played out in all areas of my life: with friends, family, relationships, my career, and even social situations. I was terrified of saying no to anything or anyone for fear of rejection or loss. I couldn't bear the thought of disappointing anyone, so I would frequently go along with whatever was being asked of me, even if it meant sacrificing my well-being.

I avoided having difficult and uncomfortable conversations because I didn't want to rock the boat, so instead, I tiptoed around on eggshells. I agreed to social events I didn't want to attend because I was scared of being left out or losing friendships, a feeling that took me back to my days at school where I had no choice but to miss out with the amount of absence I had due to so much illness.

The mental and emotional cost of this behaviour over time was excruciating.

I often felt resentful, angry, and drained. I felt suppressed and unable to express my emotions because I had conditioned myself to believe that other people's happiness was of far greater importance than my own. The more I said yes to others, the further I drifted from my true self. Over time, I realised that I had become a version of myself that was constructed by others' expectations of me rather than reflecting my true desires and values.

People-pleasing doesn't develop in a vacuum.

Often, it's a learned behaviour that stems from our upbringing, past experiences, and sometimes trauma. In many cases, it can be a survival mechanism—a way to navigate difficult or painful situations by keeping the peace and ensuring that we remain in others' good graces.

For those who have experienced trauma or loss, people-pleasing can become an especially pronounced coping strategy, as it did for me. Also referred to as 'fawning,' this is when you unconsciously 'people please' and say yes when you feel no.

Fawning is a psychological response to a perceived threat in which a person tries to appease or please someone to avoid conflict, criticism, or even harm. Along with fight, flight, and freeze, it's considered a trauma response.

This response often involves behaviours like prioritising others' needs, desires, or feelings over your own to maintain harmony, avoiding saying "no" or expressing your own preferences, agreeing with others or hiding your true feelings to avoid confrontation, and frequently saying "sorry" to prevent others from being upset or angry.

This response typically develops in people who have experienced situations where they felt powerless, such as in abusive relationships, childhood trauma, or dysfunctional family dynamics. It becomes a survival strategy to maintain safety by avoiding conflict.

When you lose someone you love or go through a traumatic event, it can shatter your sense of security and self-worth. To regain a sense of control, you may begin to overcompensate by making yourself indispensable to others. You tell yourself that if you can just keep everyone else happy, you'll be safe from further pain or rejection.

In my case, after the loss of my mother, I felt an overwhelming need to make sure everyone else in my life was happy because I couldn't bear the thought of the loss or rejection that may be the alternative. I wanted to be seen as the person who could hold everything together, even if it meant putting my own needs last. I thought that by saying yes to everyone else, I could avoid the loneliness and isolation that came with grief and loss.

But people-pleasing, I found from experience, to be a double-edged sword.

While it may provide temporary relief, like ultra-processed foods and alcohol, it can ultimately leave us

feeling deeply disconnected from ourselves. It also reinforces the belief that our worth is tied to how well we
can meet others' expectations rather than inherent in
who we are.

Society, particularly in the case of women, places
immense and immeasurable pressure on us to be everything to everyone. From a young age, we are taught to
be nurturing, accommodating, and self-sacrificing. We're
told that it's our job to take care of others, to be polite,
and to avoid confrontation at all costs. And when we do
assert ourselves—when we dare to say no or set boundaries for ourselves—we're often labeled as difficult,
high-maintenance, or even selfish.

This pressure is especially intense in social situations.
Women are expected to be agreeable, accept every invitation, and participate fully in social rituals like eating
and drinking. If we decline, we can be deemed rude or
ungrateful. If we say no to a task or responsibility, we're
viewed as shirking our duties. It's no wonder that so
many women struggle to say no, even when they're overwhelmed, exhausted, or simply uninterested.

The societal expectation that women must always be
accommodating creates a culture of guilt and shame
around saying no. We're often made to feel that if we set
boundaries, we're somehow failing in our roles as care-
givers, friends, or partners. But the truth is, saying no is
not a failure in your ability—it's an act of self-respect
and self-care.

Setting and following through on boundaries is one of
the most powerful ways to reclaim your life and start

living authentically. Boundaries allow you to say no to the things that don't serve you and yes to the things that do. They create space for you to prioritise your own needs rather than constantly putting others first.

When you start to set boundaries with yourself—like not eating the cake when you don't want it or not saying yes to every social invitation just because you're afraid of missing out—you begin to cultivate a stronger sense of self-discipline and self-worth. You learn that it's okay to prioritise your well-being, even if it means at the risk of sometimes disappointing others.

Once you establish these internal boundaries, it becomes easier to set external ones with others. When you have a firm understanding of what you need and what you're willing to tolerate, you can communicate those boundaries clearly and confidently. You can say no to requests that drain your energy or decline invitations that don't align with your values.

In my own life, learning to set boundaries was initially a challenging process because of how ingrained my behaviours around this were, but it was one of the most transformative things I've ever done.

It meant learning to say no to the stollen cake, even if it momentarily disappointed my father. It meant having uncomfortable conversations with friends and partners about what I was and wasn't willing to accept in our relationships. And it meant acknowledging that my worth was not dependent on how well I could meet others' needs but rather on my ability to honour my own.

One of the biggest obstacles to setting boundaries, which I initially found, is the fear of missing out (FOMO) or social rejection. We often worry that if we say no to social invitations, we'll be left out or that our friends will stop including us in plans. This fear can be paralysing, and it often leads us to say yes to things we don't want to do.

But the truth is, saying no doesn't have to mean social exclusion. Setting boundaries in all your relationships can lead to deeper, more authentic connections. When you stop agreeing to things out of fear or obligation, you create space for relationships based on mutual respect and understanding. You begin to attract people who value you for who you are rather than what you can do for them.

It's also important to add and remember that you are not responsible for other people's reactions to your boundaries. If someone chooses to exclude you because you said no to one event or request, in my experience, it's often a reflection of their own insecurities, not your worth. True friends and loved ones will respect your need for boundaries and understand that saying no doesn't mean you don't value the relationship—it simply means you're taking care of yourself.

Finally, I feel strongly it is time to redefine what it means to be polite.

Politeness doesn't have to mean saying yes to everything that's offered to you or putting others' needs above your own. True politeness is about being respectful and kind to others while also being truly authentic to who you are.

In many cultures, saying no is seen as rude or disrespectful, particularly when it comes to food. We're taught that it's impolite to refuse something that someone has prepared for us or to decline a request for help. But this kind of politeness often comes at the expense of your own health and well-being.

It's time to challenge this notion and recognise that it is possible to be polite while still honouring your boundaries. You can graciously decline a piece of cake or a glass of wine or say no to a social event without being rude. I have found from my personal experience the outcome is mostly defined by how you communicate your decision. A simple "Thank you, but I'm not hungry right now" or "I appreciate the invite, but I am taking some time for myself this weekend" is both polite and yet assertive.

When you stop saying yes to things you don't want, you start living your true life—not the version of life that others have placed on you. You begin to make choices that align with your values, desires, and goals rather than out of obligation or fear. And in doing so, you reclaim your power, your health, and ultimately your happiness.

Saying no is one of the most loving things you can do for yourself.

It's a declaration that your needs, your well-being, and your authentic self are worthy of respect. By setting boundaries, you take control of your life and begin to live in alignment with who you truly are rather than who others expect you to be.

As you move forward on this journey, remember that saying no is not about rejecting others—it's about embracing yourself. Honouring yourself in this way creates the space for deeper, more meaningful relationships, greater health, and a more fulfilling life.

Saying no is not just a boundary—it's an act of self-love, and it's also a full sentence that needs no further explanation.

Chapter Five

Becoming Your Own Ally - The Power of Self-Cheering and Neuroplasticity

"The hardest battle you will ever
fight is the one against yourself."

– Unknown

This saying will resonate with you, especially if you have spent a lifetime struggling to break free from the chains of self-doubt, self-sabotage, and limiting beliefs.

For many women, this internal battle can be a daily fight, as I discovered for myself. We're often our own harshest critics, sabotaging our best efforts with an inner voice that tells us we aren't good enough or words to that effect! That we will fail or that someone else's success only highlights our own inadequacies.

I know this journey only too well, both personally and professionally. The good news is that it is possible to shift from being your own worst enemy to becoming your greatest ally. It takes work, understanding your mind, and absolutely reprogramming your brain's patterns through neuroplasticity, which I have incorporated into my science-backed Unconventional Weight Loss programs.

But first, let me take you back to my own story.

My Journey to Transformation

So often, people think that when someone undergoes a transformation in any area of their life, there must have been a pivotal moment that caused this turnaround. I have frequently been asked this question in recent years. However, I can confirm that in my own transformation journey, there wasn't one defining moment, a catalyst, but rather varying sequences of events that triggered not only the desire for change but, *this* time, ultimately, the need and want for change.

Wanting, I have come to realise, and *doing* are two entirely different things.

In 2013, I remember feeling deeply unfulfilled in my corporate career, a career I had already poured nearly twenty years of my life into and, for the most part, had loved, but it had shaped my identity to a point I no longer knew who I was or felt in alignment with my evolving values. At this same point in my career, I had my first proper encounter with personal development when the global organisation I was employed by at the time hired an external behaviourist to train and coach a proportion of the company's employees. Myself being one of them.

I remember the words said to me in one of our follow-up sessions: "Naomi, no one is coming to save you." I won't deny that it was an uncomfortable concept and words that, looking back, I wasn't truly ready to hear.

Because deep down, in many ways, I *had* always been looking for someone to save me. I felt that having dealt with so many obstacles in my life, so much heartache and struggles from a young age; I somehow deserved to be saved and live an easier life. I relied heavily on the National Health Service for years to save me from my ongoing health problems; looking back, a lot of these were brought on and subsequently made increasingly worse by my choice of lifestyle habits.

I grew up watching films in which the prince always saved the princess, and I always hoped a prince would come and save me, too.

In 2015, I found myself at yet another painful cross-roads. Just a few days after my thirty-ninth birthday, I was caught in a time of deep reflection for the year ahead with a milestone birthday looming. I had a deep feeling of shame that I had reached this point in my life. I finally dared to admit to myself how unhappy I really was with my weight, my continuous poor physical and mental health, and the fact I didn't like the way I looked and, more importantly, had come to feel.

I felt trapped in a body that I was desperate to escape and in a cycle of self-sabotage. Despite years of attempting an enormity of diets, fitness plans, and one fad or another, nothing had seemed to stick.

I'd start with good intentions, and make a little progress, only to fall back into all my old bad habits—comfort eating, drinking alcohol to excess, late nights, skipping workouts, or simply giving up when life threw another curveball and I felt too overwhelmed to give my weight and health the focus it needed. The frustration was immense, and it felt like I was caught in an endless loop.

Out of sheer desperation with my ongoing weight battles, I seriously considered and researched weight loss surgery as I felt it had to be the only solution to my problem.

I now know that my weight was *not* the problem; it was merely a symptom of so many other problems I had: my low self-esteem, my lack of belief in myself, my self-sabotage, my people-pleasing tendencies, and my own fixed mindset.

I *was* the problem, and I know for me, weight loss surgery would never have been the right solution.

It wasn't until I began researching how lasting, sustainable change occurs that I realised I had missed my mindset and the science-backed behaviour change process.

It wasn't the diets or the fitness routines that were failing me, although they were all completely unsustainable and, if I'm honest, boring as hell!

I could not reshape the deep-rooted identity, thought patterns, and habits that had been ruling my life for years. I was fighting against myself every step of the way, and it wasn't until I started my self-development journey and truly understood the power of neuroplasticity and the brain's ability to change that those thoughts finally began to shift for me.

This journey was no longer about learning how to count calories or exercise more; it was about fundamentally rewiring the way I thought about myself, my capabilities, my complex relationship with food, and the life I had come to live.

I chose to learn how to become my own ally, to cheer myself on when no one else was there to do it, and to silence the critical, self-sabotaging voice that had resided in my mind for what felt like an entire lifetime.

My 64lbs weight loss came through making simple yet significant changes to my lifestyle. Once I reduced all the ultra-processed food and alcohol I was consuming, I finally started to see clearer; I could be more subjective and start to identify the triggers, behaviours, and habits that had been ingrained and controlling me for so many years.

In 2016, over four stone lighter, four dress sizes smaller, and with a glimmer of newfound confidence, I decided to set myself a physical challenge.

For years I had watched on as friends and work peers had completed various fitness challenges, often feeling a sense that I was missing out. It was around this time an advert popped up on my social media for "Dirty Dozen" a military-style obstacle course race in the South East of England. Instead of my previous style of overthinking something and telling myself I shouldn't bother signing up because I would only fail, I took the leap and signed up there and then for the 12k race.

The 20k felt like a step too far! I only said a 'glimmer' of newfound confidence. I won't deny that I had plenty of doubts and fears for the day, only enhanced when my supporters pulled out shortly before, and I was faced with going along and participating alone, something I would never have felt I could do previously when I was so self-conscious and crippled with such a fear of judgment.

As the day approached, I felt a cocktail of emotions: fear of the unknown, fear of failure, and anxiety. However, I felt an overriding excitement at the thought of achieving something I had never previously attempted, and that's what I chose to focus on.

The day came and went, mostly in a muddy, wet haze, but I was thrilled to complete the 12k race plus the extra distance by taking a wrong turn and heading down the 20k route at some point! I got my all-important finisher t-shirt, medal, and photo, but the greatest thing I received was an overwhelming feeling of accomplishment and pride.

The young girl who had always been picked last for every school sports team had finally triumphed in this race!

Within days of completing the race, with bruises still fresh across my aching body, I signed up for my next race. Over the next few years, this weekend hobby continued as I completed various obstacle course races across the South of England and collected a plethora of finisher t-shirts and medals, which I proudly hung in my home.

A forced hiatus occurred in 2020 when the global pandemic stopped all these races. For the next few years, I redirected the additional focus and time to my coaching business and juggling the ever-growing demands of everyday life.

In 2022, I felt the itch to give myself a further challenge, this time something that would challenge me to a completely different level.

Working on my mindset and overcoming old beliefs had given me a feeling of 'what else might be possible'. I made it known to friends I was looking to take on a new challenge, and when the opportunity arose in October of that year to join an expedition team to climb Mont Blanc the following year, I didn't hesitate. I didn't ask one single question about what was required; I just knew that I would give it everything I had, and that's exactly what I did. Over seven months of training sessions in North and South Wales, climbing multiple mountains, abseiling, rock climbing, and scrambling.

All things I could never even have imagined myself doing previously.

In August 2023, I headed to Chamonix-Mont-Blanc for my first expedition. Crossing glaciers and crevasses for the first time, I spent seven days climbing, hiking, and acclimatising to the altitude in preparation. I experienced the highest cable cars in France and crossed into the Aosta Valley in Italy at an altitude of 3,375 meters. On the day of our ascent, unfortunately, I did not conquer the summit of Mont Blanc; however, I overcame parts of my mind I never thought possible. Some may see it as a failure to train so long and intensely only to fall short, but a valuable lesson I have learned over the last few years is that success is rarely found in the outcome; it is found in the journey and the metaphorical mountains you climb along the way. Fresh from the disappointment, I quickly decided to turn that loss into a triumph. Forty-eight hours later, I was heading up on my own in a cable car to Le Brevent in the Aiguilles Rouges range of the French Prealps, completing my first (who knows if it will be my last!) tandem paraglide at an altitude of over 2500m. It was terrifying and exhilarating in equal measure!

I'm not going to pretend any of this was easy, that I read one book and the next day was 'reprogrammed'. My journey of trial and error, setbacks, and steps forward ultimately set me on the path to helping others.

In January 2016, at 41, I finally walked out of my twenty-one-year corporate career, a significant decision I took, I believe, to not only save my mental health but also to create a more fulfilling life for myself. For this decision some people called me crazy; some called me brave; the truth is I don't believe I was either.

I felt a deep misalignment in my life, leaving me unhappy. No matter how many weekends away I had or holidays I booked, I simply lacked a feeling of contentment.

I won't deny that it took some courage to walk away from everything I had ever known, choose a path of uncertainty, and leave the security and trimmings of a corporate job behind.

There was some fear of judgment and, of course, the thought of being seen as a failure if it didn't work out, but at that moment, all those feelings were overpowered by the deep-rooted feeling of a true need for change and being true to myself.

At this time, I started to learn to become my greatest cheerleader and ally. People asked me what my backup plan was. It was me. I *was* the backup plan, and there was no going back.

A single, independent woman with no one to fall back on but myself.

I knew that the journey I had experienced in my own weight and health had been transformative, so I felt compelled to create a way to help other women achieve this, too. This set me on the path to becoming The Unconventional Weightloss Coach.

Since then, I've had the privilege of helping hundreds of women transform their bodies, relationships, careers, confidence, and overall sense of self-worth. While weight loss has often been the initial motivator, the real transformation goes much deeper.

It's about becoming someone who no longer waits for validation from others but learns to celebrate her own victories, quiets the inner critic, and steps into her power.

But how do you go about changing the neural pathways that have kept you stuck for so long? How do you make this lasting change?

Neuroplasticity, also known as brain plasticity, is the brain's remarkable ability to change and reorganise itself and adapt by forming new neural connections. This remarkable capability allows the brain to compensate for injury, adapt to changes in the environment, and optimise cognitive functions based on experiences.

This means that your brain is not fixed as you may have previously thought; it is malleable and capable of being shaped and reshaped by your thoughts, experiences, and actions. This is incredibly powerful because it means that no matter how long you've been stuck in negative thought patterns or self-sabotaging behaviours, as I have discovered, you do have the ability to change.

Let me explain a bit further: our thoughts and behaviours create pathways in the brain, much like trails through a forest. The more we think a certain way or act out a particular behaviour, the more entrenched that pathway becomes. Over time, it becomes the default route our brain takes. This is why habits—both good and bad—are so hard to break. They are wired into your brain's architecture.

But just as a forest path can be rerouted, so too can your neural pathways. Neuroplasticity allows you to create new trails—new ways of thinking, acting, and being—by consciously choosing different thoughts and behaviours.

The key here is consistency and intention.

When I began my health transformation journey, I wasn't just changing my diet or exercising more—I was deliberately retraining my brain to think in ways that supported my goals rather than continually undermining them.

Instead of defaulting to self-criticism when I didn't meet a goal which I had done for most of my life, I practiced self-compassion and problem-solving.

Instead of giving up when things got hard, I reminded myself of my long-term vision and celebrated the smallest of wins along the way.

And that's the magic of becoming your own ally: when you consciously choose to support and cheer yourself on, regardless of what everyone around you is saying, you begin to form new neural connections that reinforce this more positive behaviour. Over time, this becomes your new default. You become someone who believes in her power, who perseveres in the face of challenges, and who celebrates her own progress—no matter how small.

That being said, before you can reprogram your brain, you must first become aware of the patterns and behaviours that are no longer serving you. This can be one of the hardest parts of the journey because it requires a deep level of honesty with yourself.

For more years than I would like to admit, I was the problem.

I found and used excuses that enabled me to feel more comfortable about my lack of action regarding my weight and health problems. I blamed my lack of time and energy, yet I always found time and energy for what was important to me at the time. I blamed a lack of resources and money, yet I found both for the things that were important to me at the time. I was constantly putting obstacles in my own way.

I'd tell myself I didn't have time to exercise, that I'd start eating better on Monday (always Monday!), or that I just needed a little treat to get through a tough day. These were all ways I was sabotaging my own success with patterns that had been ingrained for many years.

And it's not just about health or weight loss.

I've seen this same pattern play out in the lives of the women I've coached and mentored. Whether in their careers, relationships, or business ventures, the excuses and self-sabotage look strikingly similar.

You often avoid taking action because you're afraid of failing. You procrastinate because you don't believe you're truly capable of achieving what you want. You settle for less than you deserve because somewhere along the way, you've been conditioned, albeit unconsciously or consciously, to believe you're not worthy of more.

The first step in breaking free from these patterns is becoming aware of them. Start paying attention to the thoughts that arise when you face a challenge or set a goal.

Are these thoughts supportive, or are they undermining you? Are you finding reasons to take action, or are you making excuses?

Once you become aware of these patterns, you have the power to change them by rewiring your brain.

Becoming your own ally starts with an understanding of self-awareness.

You need to be able to identify the moments when you fall into old, negative patterns of thinking and behaviour. Mindfulness practices, such as meditation or journaling, can be incredibly helpful in this process. When you become more mindful, you develop the ability to observe your thoughts and actions without judgment, which gives you the power to interrupt negative patterns before they take hold.

For example, when you catch yourself thinking, "I'll never be able to do this," or "I'm not good enough," take a moment to pause and recognise that thought for exactly what it is: a well-worn neural pathway that no longer serves you. Then, consciously choose a different thought—one that is more supportive and aligned with your future goals.

The thoughts you think repeatedly will indeed create your reality. This is why affirmations and visualisation are such powerful tools for helping to reprogramme the brain. When you repeatedly tell yourself positive, empowering things, you are creating new neural connections that support these beliefs.

On my transformation journey, I made a conscious effort to replace negative self-talk with affirmations. Instead of telling myself, "I'll never be able to lose this weight," I began affirming, "I am capable of creating lasting change in my life." Instead of focusing on past failures, I visualised myself achieving my goals, feeling strong, healthy, and confident in the body I was creating.

This practice wasn't just about "positive thinking"—something I had been told to adopt many times when I was struggling with my mental health over the years.

It was about retraining my brain to believe in my power. And over time, those affirmations became my reality.

One of the most powerful things you can do to become your ally is to celebrate your progress—no matter how small. When we only focus on the end goal and the outcome, it's easy to become discouraged and give up. But when we take the time to acknowledge and celebrate each small victory along the way, we start to build momentum and reinforce the neural pathways that support our success.

When I was working on my health transformation, I didn't wait until I reached my healthy goal weight to celebrate. I celebrated every day I committed to being more active, every healthy meal I chose, and every time I said no to something that didn't feel aligned with me. Each small win reminded me that I was making progress, and it gave me a little more confidence and belief to keep going.

The same applies to any area of your life.

Whether you're working on improving your career, relationships, or personal growth, take the time to acknowledge and celebrate the small steps you're taking in the right direction. This will help you build the confidence and momentum you need to keep moving forward, especially when you have setbacks.

Embracing Self-Compassion

Becoming an ally also means learning to be kind to yourself, especially when things go awry. We are all human, and we will all make mistakes or fall short of our goals at times. What matters is how we respond to those moments.

In the past, when I would slip up on my health goals, I'd be incredibly hard on myself. I'd spiral into negative self-talk and often end up giving up entirely. But when I learned how to practice self-compassion, everything changed. Instead of berating myself for a bad day, I reminded myself that setbacks are a natural part of the process. I acknowledged my humanity and made a plan to get back on track without the need for any shame or guilt.

Equally, I previously had a natural tendency to want to be too lenient on myself; I dressed it up as 'self-care' and not being too hard on myself by letting myself have the cake, the takeaway, and the glass of wine to feel better every time my thoughts told me I wanted them but in fact, I couldn't differentiate between self-sabotage and self-compassion back then, it was a blurred line.

This mindset shift is crucial for long-term success. When you learn to treat yourself with the same kindness and understanding you would offer a friend, you become your own greatest source of support.

One of the most profound lessons I've learned on this journey is that real, lasting change isn't just about changing your habits—it's about reshaping your identity. This sounds scarier than it is and doesn't involve an *actual* change of identity!

However, who you believe you are at your core will always dictate the actions you take and the results you achieve.

For years, I continuously saw myself as someone who struggled with her weight, someone who wasn't disciplined or successful in maintaining healthy habits. And as long as I held that identity, my day-to-day actions continued to reflect it.

I'd start strong with tons of motivation to change but inevitably fall back into old patterns because, deep down, I didn't believe I was capable or worthy of real change.

It wasn't until I started to shift my identity—seeing myself as someone healthy, more disciplined, and capable of achieving the goals she set herself—that everything started to change.

I stopped approaching weight loss as something I had to "try" and started acting like the person I wanted to become. I made decisions from the mindset of someone already living a healthier lifestyle, and over time, that has become my reality.

If you want to become your own ally and create lasting change in any area of your life, you must start by reshaping your identity. You must stop seeing yourself as someone who struggles, sabotages, or isn't good enough. Instead, start seeing yourself as the person you want to become. Embody that identity in your thoughts, actions, and decisions, and watch as your reality shifts.

One of the most liberating realisations you can have is that you don't need anyone else to cheer you on—you have the power to be your own greatest cheerleader. When you stop waiting for external validation or support, you reclaim your power and become the driving force behind your success.

I've worked with countless women who, like me, spent years waiting for others to motivate them, support them, or cheer them on. Whether it was a partner, a friend, or a family member, they believed they needed someone else to push them to succeed. But the truth is that external support of the right kind is vital to putting you on the right path. Real, lasting change comes from within.

This an important reminder that "No one is coming to save you."

When you learn to quiet the negative self-talk and replace it with words of encouragement and self-belief, you unlock a new level of motivation and resilience. You no longer need to rely on others to keep you going because you've become your source of support.

Yes, I am human, and there are still times when I have thoughts of self-doubt or self-sabotage that may lead me to momentarily fall back into old patterns. But the difference now is that I have the tools and awareness to recognise when this happens and to course-correct without beating myself up.

I've become my own greatest ally and cheerleader, and that has made all the difference in my life.

Becoming your own ally is not an overnight process.

It takes time, commitment, and a willingness to face your deepest limiting beliefs and maybe some fears. But it is one of the most empowering and transformative journeys you can embark on.

When you take responsibility for your own success, learn to cheer yourself on, and harness the power of neuroplasticity to reprogram your brain, you unlock a limitless potential within yourself.

You become someone who doesn't just achieve her goals but someone who believes in her worth, who takes action despite fear, and who celebrates her progress every step of the way.

If I can make this change, so can you. You have every-thing you need within you to become your own greatest ally and cheerleader.

So start today—one thought, one action, one moment at a time—and watch as your life begins to transform in ways you never thought possible.

Chapter Six

Your New Narrative Begins Now

As I write this final chapter of *your new narrative*, I reflect on my own journey—the winding and somewhat turbulent path that has led me to a place of health, peace, and purpose.

For many years, I felt trapped in a body and mind that constantly struggled.

Ongoing health issues with viral and bacterial infections, chronic back pain, asthma, long bouts of depression, and deep anxiety seemed to define my very existence.

Taking control and being happy with my weight felt like an impossible task.

Emotional eating controlled my days and nights, and I often felt disconnected from every part of myself. The numerous medications I heavily relied on became a part of my identity, as did the overwhelming feeling that something was missing—that I wasn't truly living the life I was meant to live.

Yet, through all those challenges, I discovered a deeper truth: I had the power to change my story, to reclaim my health and my life. And so do you.

For years, I viewed my poor health as something that happened to me.

It was like a series of unfortunate events that I had little control over. But over time, I began to realise that, ultimately, I did have a choice in how I responded to my circumstances. I may not have been able to control the fact that I had chronic pain or that my body seemed prone to infections, but I could take steps to support my health, strengthen my body, and build resilience.

This shift in mindset and identity didn't happen overnight. It was a process—one that involved some deep honesty with myself, a lot of trial and error, learning and unlearning, and, most importantly, tuning into what my body and mind truly needed. The culmination and impact of this journey led me to create and develop my own method: the S.M.A.R.T Formula. This unique formula has enabled me to become pain-free, medication-free, and depression-free and navigate the transition into menopause more holistically and agreeably.

It gave me the power to reclaim my physical, mental, and emotional health and my life in ways I never thought possible.

The S.M.A.R.T. Formula is your personal gateway to liberation from the constraints of dieting and emotional eating, all while enjoying the foods and beverages you cherish!

S.M.A.R.T is an acronym for Sleep, Mindful Nutrition, Activity, Rest and Recovery, and Time for Self. Each of these pillars has played a crucial role in my healing process, and I believe they can be equally transformative for you.

The S.M.A.R.T Formula isn't just another checklist of things to do in your already overstretched day; it's a way of living that honours your body, mind, and soul.

Sleep: It all starts with sleep. Without adequate, quality sleep, your body cannot heal, your mind cannot focus, and your emotions become harder to manage. I learned the hard way that burning the candle at both ends and sacrificing sleep in the name of productivity or pleasure only set me back further. By prioritising sleep, I began to notice improvements in my energy levels, my mood, and even my immune system. Quality sleep became my foundation for optimal health and took me from years of insomnia to deep and restorative sleep.

Mindful Nutrition: For years, I struggled with emotional eating. Food was my comfort in times of stress, loneliness, and sadness, and equally, it became my pleasure in times of celebration, but it only left me feeling worse in the long run. I knew I needed to change my complex relationship with food, not just to lose weight but to nourish my body in a way that supported healing it too. I became more mindful of the foods I was eating, choosing nutrient-dense options that fuelled my body rather than the ultra-processed foods that had previously depleted it. I explored the root causes of my dieting habits, restrictive eating patterns, and emotional eating whilst reprogramming my neural pathways to create healthier, sustainable habits.

This shift helped me manage my weight, but more importantly, it helped me feel more connected to myself.

Activity: Movement became an essential part of my recovery, not just physically but mentally and emotionally. Gentle daily activities, such as walking, allowed me to reconnect with my body and release tension. I stopped punishing myself with intense, grueling and unsustainable workouts and instead focused on activities that felt good and nurtured my health. Over time, my body has become stronger, more resilient, and more capable, enabling me to become increasingly active.

Rest and Recovery: Rest is not just about sleeping. It's about giving yourself permission to slow down and recover, both physically and emotionally. For women entering menopause, in particular, rest and recovery are crucial. Hormonal changes can leave you feeling depleted, and the everyday demands of modern-day life can make it difficult to cope. However, by taking time to rest and recharge, you can navigate this vulnerable stage with grace and strength. I learned to listen to my body's cues and permit myself to rest when needed without guilt or shame.

Time for Self: Perhaps the most important part of the S.M.A.R.T Formula is making time for yourself. As women, we often put everyone else's needs before our own, but self-care is not selfish; it's essential. For me, making time for myself meant carving out moments for reflection and to just BE. It also meant setting boundaries and learning to say "no" to things that didn't serve me. By prioritising this all-important time for myself, alongside juggling the demands of everyday life, I have been able to reconnect with my inner voice and rediscover what truly mattered to me.

Through the consistency of these five key pillars, I was able to break free from the cycle of dieting, a disordered relationship with my food and my body, to reclaim my health, my confidence, and my life. I no longer rely on any medications to manage my health, I am free from chronic pain, and I no longer struggle with depression or anxiety. My journey wasn't easy, but it was worth every step. And I know that if I can do it, so can you.

The S.M.A.R.T. Formula has not only worked for me but also helped hundreds of women transform their lives.

Women who, just like you, were once struggling to manage their health and weight, feeling stuck in a narrative they didn't want to live anymore.

Here are a few of their stories to inspire you and show you how the S.M.A.R.T formula can change your life, too:

"I first approached Naomi to see if she could help me get my diabetes under control, but she has given me so much more than I ever expected. She has helped me discover a love for walking, overcome my fear of going underwater, and enjoy cold water swimming.

Also to understand that so much of life is about your mindset. I've learned to quiet the negative voices in my head and make better choices. I've also established healthy boundaries in both my business and personal life, which has transformed everything beyond recognition. I'm now happier and healthier than I have been in years.

Naomi has created an incredible community of strong, supportive women where we not only uplift one another but form lasting friendships. I was honoured to attend her first in-person event, which was such a special and unforgettable day that none of us wanted it to end. Thanks to her guidance, I now have the confidence to embark on a new and exciting chapter of my life, following her inspiring example and striving to be the best version of myself. I'm truly grateful for everything she's done for me, and I do not regret investing in myself. So excited to read her first book and see how she continues to help many more women, who need her guidance and support."

— Judi, 53

"I have finally set myself free from a life dictated by food.

It is truly the easiest formula there is. It will help you gain control of your whole life.

My confidence has skyrocketed, and I have managed to release two stones of excess fat that I never thought I could get rid of. I have heaps of energy, which has been absolutely fantastic, so I can keep up with my energetic ten-year-old daughter. I have finally said goodbye to antidepressants.

I can honestly say the S.M.A.R.T formula has changed my life. I will always be grateful for the day I met Naomi and for her S.M.A.R.T formula."

— Tanya, 43

"I was completely lost.

Suffering from extremely low mood, feeling tired, angry, sad, anxious, no energy, being overweight, grieving the loss of both parents, going through menopause, which has negatively impacted my life massively, suffering from psoriasis badly, and using cream daily, on anti-depressants for five years, aches and pains in legs were severe, my relationship with my husband was under terrible strain, using alcohol as a coping tool, becoming isolated from friends and family as I tried to work a way through how I was feeling! I'd wake up dreading the day ahead and wondering how I'd get through it, just going through the motions every single day. I was literally 'stuck' and couldn't see the future clearly at all.

I can say without a doubt that joining this program and working with Naomi was one of the best decisions I have ever made.

I took action, and now I'm feeling fabulous.

Everything's changed: my mood has lifted, I have bags of energy, my skin is so much healthier, and I no longer use the psoriasis cream; I'm completely off the anti-depressants, built up resilience to tackle my menopause and aches and pains in legs now minimal, learned to limit alcohol and sweet sugary foods, I've released three stones in weight and maintained it, and I wake up with a new positive outlook on the days ahead. I'd forgotten how it felt to feel happy inside, I feel GREAT! I'm not just smiling on the outside; I'm smiling on the inside again.

In such a short time, I can't believe the huge change in me.

It's a lifestyle change and not just a quick fix. It's tailored to my individual needs and daily commitments. I don't feel hungry or deprived of food or drinks. It gives aware-ness of midlife changes and how to success-fully adapt our bodies to deal with this time in our lives, concerning food choices and nutrients that are essential to my health and happiness. Naomi is supportive in every imaginable way. The Inner Circle Community members are also key to the success of this whole program, sharing experiences, feel-ings, food tips, and ideas, daily sharing of ups and downs, and how their journeys are progressing. This is incredibly reassuring and encouraging to know you're not alone.

I've realised how important sleep is to my well-being, and I'm mentally & physically stronger.

My everyday lifestyle has completely changed. I go out walking in nature every single day. I've challenged myself to step out of my comfort zone, successfully completing a 5k, and now I go running every week. I'm also facing my fear of water and attending swimming lessons.

Naomi has equipped me with all the tools I need to lead a healthy, happy, and positive life in the next chapter. I've learned to navi-gate each challenge I encounter.

It feels like the first time in my life that I've nourished my body and mind. Now, I under-stand what my body needs to thrive.

Naomi has helped me to take back control of my life."

— Maxine, 54

"Before working with Naomi, I was stuck in a cycle of eating for the sake of it—never truly enjoying my food and confused by all the diet rules I'd tried over the years.

I thought I knew it all after trying Slimming World and Weight Watchers, but nothing clicked.

Naomi completely transformed my perspective on food, teaching me that what I put into my body is my fuel for life.

Her S.M.A.R.T formula helped me understand that proper nutrition, along with quality sleep, regular routines, and daily movement, is key to living positively.

Now, I wake up each day feeling motivated and focused, and I've found joy in both my personal and professional life.

Naomi's coaching has not only changed how I eat but has helped me become the best version of myself. I'm so grateful for her guidance!"

— Kirstie, 48

"I was quite far along on my transformation journey when I started working with Naomi and using the S.M.A.R.T formula. However, I feel that Naomi's approach has had a huge impact in cementing my habits. As Naomi says, diets often don't work, and without the idea of changing my mindset, too, I may not have maintained the changes. I am hugely grateful to have had the chance to work with Naomi. I started looking after myself more due to hormonal changes that were affecting me so severely, and I wanted to take back control. But what I didn't understand was that it takes more than just physical changes to make a difference. I needed to start changing my mindset and actually become this new, healthier, happier version of myself, mentally as well as physically. This is what working with Naomi has supported me to do. And I can honestly say I am happier than I have been for years and possibly in the best physical health that I have ever been in."

— Lizi, 54

The Time to Take Action Is Now

If there's one overriding message I wish you to take away from this book and our journey together, it's that you have the power to change your story right here, right now. I know that it's easy to wait for the "right" moment—the moment when all the circumstances in your life are perfect, when the stars align, and it feels like the ideal time to make a change.

But the truth is, there is no perfect moment.

You get to create it.

Life will always present challenges. There will always be reasons to put off taking care of yourself, whether it's work, family responsibilities, or simply feeling too over-whelmed to begin. But waiting for that perfect moment means delaying your own happiness, healing, and trans-formation.

The moment to start is now.

You don't need to wait for another Monday or the start of a new month or year. You can now decide that today is the day you begin writing your new narrative.

You might be wondering, "Where do I even begin?"

The answer is simpler than you think: start with small, simple, manageable steps. You don't need to overhaul your entire life overnight. Begin by incorporating one aspect of the S.M.A.R.T Formula into your routine—maybe it's prioritising sleep, taking a little time for yourself each day, or making small changes to be more mindful of your nutrition.

Each small step you take is a step toward reclaiming your health and rewriting your story.

As you begin your journey, I want you to know that you are not alone.

I've been where you are, and so have the many women I've worked with. We've felt the same frustration, the same fear, the same self-doubt as you are feeling currently. We've felt trapped in bodies that don't feel like our own. We've felt trapped in our bad habits. But we've also experienced the joy of transformation, the empowerment of taking control of our health, and the deep sense of peace that comes with living in alignment with our true selves.

You have everything you need within you to create your unique formula for health and happiness. You are capable of transforming your life, of reclaiming your health, and of becoming the best version of yourself.

And if you ever need support or guidance along the way, remember I'm here for you.

The Unconventional Weightloss Coach

As The Unconventional Weightloss Coach, my mission is to help women like you rewrite your story and reclaim your life, starting with your weight and your health. If you want to learn more about how we can work together, you can find me at:

www.theunconventionalweightlosscoach.com

As I close, I want to leave you with this all-important last thought: you are the author of your own story. You have the power to create a new narrative, to break free from the patterns and beliefs that no longer serve you, and to step into a life that is aligned with who you truly are.

The journey ahead may not always be easy, but it will be worth it.

You will face some challenges along the way, but you will also experience many moments of joy, growth, and transformation. As you begin to rewrite your story, you will discover strengths and possibilities within yourself that you never knew existed.

Your new narrative is waiting to be written, and it starts today.

Thank you for joining me on this journey.

I can't wait to see where your new narrative takes you.

Wishing you good health, happiness, and freedom.

Manufactured by Amazon.ca
Bolton, ON

44666241R00079